Endorsements from Ministry, Industry, and Academia

An African proverb intimates that "the Spirit cannot descend without a song." So it remains the case for the Black Churches and the Black worship experience today. Dr. Antonia Arnold-McFarland has written a powerful volume that speaks to the contemporary needs and future prospects of music and worship arts ministry in the Black Church. Through exhaustive scholarly research and grounded in her vast experience as a practitioner in the areas of worship leadership and choral direction, Dr. Arnold-McFarland addresses many of the dynamics that will affect the Black worship experience into the future, and she offers prescriptive, practical insight as to how worship experiences can be enhanced in years to come. Her work is must-read material for church and worship leaders serving in Black church contexts.

Anthony Hunt, Ph.D.,
Professor and Distinguished Lecturer of Theology, St. May's Seminary and University, Baltimore, MD,
Author of *Keep Looking Up: Sermons on the Psalms.*

* * *

Dr. Antonia Arnold-McFarland's research in *The Evolution of African American Worship* is a useful "how-to and go-to handbook" for pastors, music ministers and departments of Christian Education. It will be useful for those who must provide *balanced*, meaningful, spirit-filled music from the entire Black Sacred Music experience which ranges from the field songs, anthemic concertized Negro Spirituals, metered hymns, shaped note-singing, hymns of improvisation and classical anthems to traditional, modern traditional, contemporary which includes modern contemporary, urban and inspirational gospel music styles, praise and worship and Christian Contemporary Music (CCM). The in-depth attention to the various styles of worship and the sounds which emanated from those varied styles will only enhance one's worship experience, creating an atmosphere that empowers the minister or director of music to glorify **GOD**, edify and inspire **HIS** people to break chains and change conditions of their lived situations.

Professor L. Stanley Davis, Black Sacred Music Historian
Affiliations include
Northwestern University, Dept. of African American Studies, School of Music
Loyola University Chicago, Program of African American Studies, Music Program of the Fine Arts Dept.
DePaul University School of Music
Associate Editor of the *African American Heritage Hymnal*
G.I.A. Publications, Inc.

* * *

The profound research garnered in "The Evolution of African American Worship" is an extraordinary contribution paramount in the development and growth of the 21st century black church. The by-product of this massive research, "Moving Forward and Facing the Future" is also a crucial resource pertinent in navigating effective music ministry. I was honored to perform in the Lecture/demonstration of this work, which provided a moving overview of its historical content.

Dr. Arnold-McFarland, a brilliant engineer and musician, has coalesced parts of both disciplines to produce a superb source that is sure to transform those who consume its content.

I highly recommend it for music ministry staffs seeking evolution, but particularly those in academia as it is comprehensive and effectively presents the historical, addresses common issues, provides solutions and an essential plan of action for moving forward.

Valerie D. Johnson,
Vocal Maestra, Clinician, Choral Director, Greensboro, NC
Board of Directors, Hymns for Him, Inc.
Board of Directors, High Point Community Concerts Association

Master of Music in Vocal Performance, Howard University
University Faculty, Music Professor, NC A&T State University
Bennet College (affiliation)

Author, *"Wow! I needed to Know that!"*

* * *

The Gospel Music Workshop of America, Inc. is honored, pleased and proud to have Dr. Antonia Arnold McFarland as an Instructor, Administrator and highly respected Lecturer in African-American music. As evidenced in your printed and published materials, you are a great asset to this organization as we continue to build upon our Research and Developments in African-American History and Sacred Music experiences. We look forward to a lasting relationship with you!

Rt. Rev. Dr. Albert L. Jamison Sr.,
Chair, Board of Directors

Dr. Charles F. Reese, Dean & Vice Chair Academics
Gospel Music Workshop of America, Inc.

* * *

It is with pleasure that we embrace the literary work of Dr. Antonia Arnold-McFarland, a newly appointed member of the Board of Directors of Hymns for Him, Inc. Hymns for Him, Inc. is a non-profit organization created by sacred music enthusiasts with the goal of preserving and encouraging a culture of hymnody in contemporary worship. The research and passion of Dr. Arnold-McFarland is an invaluable asset to the work of Hymns for Him. She is committed to the discovery and exploration of the vital contributions of African American composers and musicians to sacred music within the worship experience. We are excited and anticipate many years of collaboration with Dr. Arnold-McFarland and her research in the area of African American worship.

Warm Regards.

Dr. David L. Allen, Sr.,
Founder President and CEO

Composer, "No Greater Love"
Recorded by G.M.W.A. National Mass Choir (Live in Miami and 25th Anniversary Album), Georgia Mass Choir, CLC Youth Choir and by various other artists

Frances Knight Thompson
Executive Director Hymns for Him, Inc.

The Evolution of African-American Worship by Dr. Antonia M. Arnold-McFarland

Copyright © 2019 by EFlat Major Productions. All rights reserved.

No portion of this book may be reproduced, stored in a retrieval system, or transmitted in any form or by any means, except for brief quotations in printed reviews, without prior permission of author. Requests may be submitted by email: eflatmaj@bellsouth.net.

Unless otherwise noted, all Scripture quotations are taken from the New King James Version®. Copyright © 1982 by Thomas Nelson. Used by permission. All rights reserved.

Scripture quotations marked KJV are taken from King James Version.

Scripture quotations marked NIV are taken from THE HOLY BIBLE, NEW INTERNATIONAL VERSION®, NIV® Copyright © 1973, 1978, 1984, 2011 by Biblica, Inc.® Used by permission. All rights reserved worldwide.

Editing services by ChristianEditingServices.com

Cover and Interior Design by dhbonner.net

PRINT ISBN: 978-1-7323365-3-7
eBOOK ISBN: 978-1-7323365-4-4

Printed in the United States of America

THE EVOLUTION OF AFRICAN-AMERICAN WORSHIP

FROM MUSIC MINISTRY TO
MUSIC INDUSTRY, AS PURSUED BY THE
INDEPENDENT GOSPEL ARTIST

FROM THE THOMAS DORSEY TO KIRK FRANKLIN ERA

Presented in Partial Fulfillment of the Requirements for
Degree of Doctor of Ministry in Creative Arts
by
Antonia Arnold-McFarland

Faculty Project Advisor
Dr. C. Anthony Hunt

The Graduate Theological Foundation
Mishawaka, Indiana
December 2015

*All requirements were met. The degree was conferred
to Dr. Arnold-McFarland in May 2016.*

DEDICATION

This work is dedicated to my mother, the late Mary F. Arnold, who was my very first music teacher for piano and voice. She believed in me more than I believed in myself. As the church organist, she accompanied me as I played the piano for my church debut. I played "Jesus Loves Me" at the age of five at Silver Hill United Methodist Church in Spartanburg, South Carolina. This moment planted a seed and passion within me for music ministry that will continue to fulfill me for the rest of my days.

This work is also dedicated to my grandmother, the late Annie Maude Mathis, and her sister, my great-aunt, the late Otis Rookard Miller. They both inspired me musically in my early years with their piano playing. My Aunt Otis helped my father cover the expense of my piano lessons after my mother passed at the untimely age of 42. This work is dedicated to my father, Raymond Arnold Jr., who still resides in Spartanburg. As my mom lay hospitalized in her last days after battling cancer for three years, he promised her that he would not allow me to quit taking piano lessons. She inspired a love for music in all three of her children. As a result of my father's commitment, her musical legacy—especially as a church musician—has been carried on through me. Thanks, Dad.

Indeed it came to pass, when the trumpeters and singers *were* as one, to make one sound to be heard in praising and thanking the Lord, and when they lifted up their voice with the trumpets and cymbals and instruments of music, and praised the Lord, *saying:*

> *"For He is good,*
> For His mercy *endure*s forever,"

that the house, the house of the Lord, was filled with a cloud, so that the priests could not continue ministering because of the cloud; for the glory of the Lord filled the house of God.

-2 Chronicles 5:13-14 NKJV

TABLE OF CONTENTS

Foreword xi

Abstract xiii

Acknowledgments xv

Music Biography 1

Chapters:

1 – Introduction 4

2 – Theological Framework 10

3 – Literature Review of the Historical Development of Gospel Music 21

    Pre-Gospel Era (Pre-1900), Pre- and Post-Emancipation Ditties, Hollers, and Spirituals 22

    Pre-Gospel Era (1900–1920), Empowerment by Education Negro Spirituals/Anthems 24

    Development (1920s–1930s) and Traditional Gospel Era (1930–1945) The Harlem Renaissance /
    New Negro Movement Gospel Hymnody/Gospel Genre 25

    Golden Age of Gospel (1945–Mid-1960s)
    1960–1967 Modern Traditional Included)
    Post-World War II 29

    Contemporary Period (Late 1960s–1970s)
    (Note: 1967 to present often referred to as the Modern Contemporary Era)
    Civil Rights Movement and Post-Civil Rights Era 33

    Modern Contemporary (late 1960s–1970s/1980s– 1990)
    Emerging Trends in Gospel 37

    Contemporary Period (1990s–2000)
    Emerging Trends in Gospel Music Business and Sound 40

    Gospel Music in the New Millennium (2000–2015) 44

4 – Research Methodology: Explication of the Analytical Approach 58

5 – Presentation and Analysis 62

6 – Summary, Improvements, and Implications of Research Recommendations for Continued Study 108

Conclusion 121

Bibliography 123

List of Tables, Figures, and Images 129

Appendix 1 133

Web Content

Gospel Music One Sound Facebook Page

Gospel Music One Sound Video Montage

Email Address: Gospel Music One Sound Project

FOREWORD

For hundreds of years African Americans have practiced and sustained a unique pattern of worship. The energy and passion found within their worship has proven to be both an amazement and anomaly to those inside and outside of the African American tradition. Yet the process of worship has transformed as much as it has been a transforming agent among African Americans. Dr. Antonia addresses the evolution of African American worship from the days of slavery through to the 21st century. By applying quantitative and qualitative methods of research she helps to provide an explanation for the energy, freedom of expression and evolution of the African American worship experience. Through assessment and analysis of the historical evolution of African American worship Arnold-McFarland has been able to offer insight and suggest practical measures for improving and sustaining this rich cultural tradition of worship.

Raymond Wise, Ph.D.
Professor of Practice, African American and African Diaspora Studies
Indiana University, Bloomington, Indiana
President, Raise Productions Center for the Gospel Arts

ABSTRACT

The African-American worship experience has evolved since its inception on American plantations up to current day multi-faceted worship styles, which include various art forms. The music component has been a major impetus in the evolution process. Gospel music has been an evolving by-product as the African-American worship experience continues to develop. Along this journey there has been a constant interchange between sacred and secular influences. At times this interchange has been highly controversial yet over time has become more collaborative.

The music ministry of the African-American worship experience originally was accessible only in the church worship space, yet the social plight of the African-American brought the opportunity to expose other cultures to gospel music as an art form. The gospel sound revolutionized by Thomas Dorsey was initially met with controversy because of the blues music influence. The social climate for justice provided a platform for gospel singers to attract listeners and to increase demand for recorded music to be available on wax or via airwaves. Additionally, the traditional Black Church worship service provided a regular venue for talented musicians and vocalists to share their gifts, have concerts, and write music for the masses. These demands gave birth to the gospel music artist, who could now pursue music as ministry as well as for income purposes.

In the music industry, music album sales (units) are a measure of business performance. A unit can be a CD (compact disc), CS (compact single), EP (3–5 songs), LP (long-play full album), or digital album. According to Nielsen ratings, a leading global information and measurement company, 257 million units sold in the US in 2014. The Christian gospel genre contributed 17.36 million units to this total. These figures have shown a steady decline since 2008. For the US, 428.4 million units sold in 2008. The Christian gospel genre alone sold 29.79 million units (Nielsen, 2014).

As a result of this trend, the Christian gospel artist, regardless of cultural focus, must compete with mainstream artists to stay relevant and to maintain market share. Urban/R&B gospel is the current categorical description of the African-American gospel artist. The category is a sub-genre included in the 17.36 million units of Christian gospel music sold in the US in 2014 (Nielsen, 2014). Gospel music artists face the challenge of aligning their ministry pursuits with biblical principles while remaining relevant in the music and entertainment industry as a whole.

This study was conducted to address the challenge faced by the independent gospel artist who desires to maintain Christian conviction while pursuing a place in the gospel music industry. It surveys the misalignments and offers solutions to aspiring artists seeking to balance ministry and industry. It provides industry awareness and knowledge to allow them to leverage the industry platform for ministry to the world. Current-day movies, plays, recordings, and reality TV shows are products within the reach of Christian artists and preachers. Although these publications are for profit, is it possible for them to still convey biblical teachings and prophesy of Christ in the mainstream pop culture arena? A trace of the historical development of the African-American worship space, embodied by gospel music, enables this study to unfold.

ACKNOWLEDGMENTS

I feel both honored and humbled to be able to serve God in any capacity. I must first acknowledge God for giving me my musical gift and for giving me a passion for worship. I thank God also for placing people in my life to shape me and to help me grow in my abilities. I give special thanks to my father, Raymond Arnold Jr.; my sister, Dr. Sonya Rae Arnold; and my brother, Raymond "Trey" Arnold III, who gave me honest feedback and support as I grew musically. Their musical abilities are gifted and inspired me to continue.

In 2005, my husband, Tony D. McFarland Sr., began providing feedback where my immediate family left off. I give special thanks to him for his support and musical wisdom and for continuing this journey with me. Together we launched an ensemble of talented vocalists and musicians called Blessed Union, The Group. Thank you to all past and present members of Blessed Union, The Group, for the miles we have travelled together spreading the gospel and for enduring the trials and triumphs with us. They contributed to my experience from which I have written, and they have been helping me with this dissertation without even knowing it. They have been my random samples, subjects for experimentation, survey participants, professors, marketing team, co-presenters, IT support, actors, caterers, ministers, prayer warriors, fellow artists, and most of all, life-long friends. Words cannot express my gratitude for their loyalty and commitment to the purpose and vision of Blessed Union, The Group.

I acknowledge all my piano instructors, especially Dr. Sheri Mitchell. I studied classical piano with her at Converse College Pre-College Music in Spartanburg as a teenager. Thank you to the choirs and music directors of my past. I give special thanks to Mrs. Betty Fowler of Upper Shady Grove Baptist Church, Wellford, South Carolina. She transcribed scores and demonstrated the patient role of a music director while nurturing me when I served as a youth choir musician. She gave me an extensive collection of gospel scores, including the works of Edwin Hawkins, Andraé Crouch, and various mass choirs of the 1980s. I give special thanks to Ron Foreman, Eleania Ward, and the New Horizons Choir Alumni of North Carolina State University. I thank them for demonstrating excellence to me and for giving me a repertoire of Negro spirituals and traditional and contemporary choir music of the 1980s and 1990s. I can still remember some of those songs more than 20 years later.

Thank you to colleagues in music ministry and academia who have worked with me in the Raleigh-Durham area and assisted with the Gospel Music One Sound Project and manuscript proofing. Thank you to the pastors of the churches who nurtured me spiritually while I served. I want to especially mention Pastor K. Ray Hill and the Maple Temple United Church of Christ family, Pastor Kenneth Pugh of the Christian Community of Hatcher Grove, and Rev. Dr. William T. Newkirk, Senior Pastor of Oak City Baptist Church. Special thanks to the Oak City Baptist church family for the facility use and donations for research. I thank Richard Jones for his technical guidance and printing services. I thank Dr. William T. Newkirk, Dr. Jean Brown, and Dr. Dorothy Burns for microediting and ongoing support. Dr. Jean Brown provided me with valuable opportunities as she pursued her doctorate, which helped prepare me for my own doctoral work. These church families, choirs, and pastors were instrumental in my academic, musical, and spiritual development. They provided me with an atmosphere for expanding my abilities that contributed to this doctoral work and my gospel music industry pursuits. I acknowledge and thank the Raleigh-Durham area chapter of the Thomas Dorsey Convention (National Convention of Gospel Choirs and Choruses, Inc. [NCGCC]) and all the musicians who have been my community colleagues in ministry. Thank you to the faculty and staff of Eastern Carolina Christian College and Seminary for providing academic support and the opportunity to develop as an instructor.

I give special thanks to Pastor William Becton of House of Worship in Charlotte, North Carolina, for extensive spiritual advising, musical nurturing, and music industry mentoring for my husband and me. His academic support in my doctoral work has been enlightening and encouraging. His discernment and wisdom have been invaluable to us.

I give thanks to all who have supported this academic process and project work at any level not already mentioned. I give special thanks to Professor L. Stanley Davis of Chicago, who is internationally renowned for his contributions in teaching black sacred music and for his work in black sacred studies at Northwestern University. He contributed to my academic undergirding on studies and scholarly work in black sacred music. He has been a consultant, subject matter expert, and tour guide through the time capsule of black sacred music and its foremost art form today as gospel music. We met at the Stellar Awards 2012 and again at the Gospel Music Workshop of America (GMWA) 2012. He has continued to help guide my field experience and industry engagement. His insight, breadth of knowledge, hands-on experience, and personal interaction with gospel legends past and present are amazing. I consider him a modern-day oracle of black sacred music and a griot in African-American culture. This is based on his lived experience in the subject and his ability to collect, interpret, clarify, and indicate the past, present, and future of the African-American worship experience, from music ministry to the gospel music industry.

Through these experiences I met Dr. Raymond Wise, whose dissertation has been a primary resource for my research. He is an amazing scholar in his own right and a professor at the African-American Arts Institute at Indiana University Bloomington. Dr. Wise imparted significant knowledge and inspiration into all who attended his lecture series on African-American Music and Worship at the Gospel Music Workshop of America in 2012. This motivated me to dig deeper and laid a framework for my project.

I am grateful for scholarly guidance, impartation, and inspiration from ethnomusicologist Dr. Birgitta Johnson of the University of South Carolina; Dr. Tony McNeill, Director of Worship and Arts at Historic Ebenezer Baptist Church in Atlanta; and Mr. Steven Ford, highly acclaimed industry producer, music consultant, and lecturer of African-American church music.

Last but not least, thank you to the faculty and staff of the Graduate Theological Foundation who have supported my academic pursuit of a doctor of ministry degree. The staff has assisted me on this journey since 2011. I especially thank Dr. C. Anthony Hunt, who helped me pace and complete the final academic requirements and ensured my experience would be well rounded. I greatly appreciate his guidance, patience, feedback, and encouragement as my project advisor. This helped to bring the best out of me. For this I am grateful.

MUSIC BIOGRAPHY

Antonia (Toni) Arnold-McFarland

Antonia Maria Arnold-McFarland is an accomplished pianist, background vocalist, and choir directress who began playing at the age of four. She came from a musical family. Her first teacher and most impactful musical influence was her mother, the late Mary F. Arnold, who was a well-known and accomplished pianist, organist, and vocalist known in the Greenville-Spartanburg area of South Carolina. Toni's paternal grandmother, the late Annie Maude Mathis, influenced her musically as she played and sang children's songs in her kindergarten in Spartanburg. After retiring from teaching, Ms. Mathis nurtured the African-American community in the 1960s and early 1970s with the only kindergarten in the area during this time for African-American children. Ms. Mathis's sister, the late Otis Rookard Miller, was a musical influence on Toni as well. She was a retired school teacher and a musician at their church, Upper Shady Grove Baptist in Wellford, South Carolina. Ms. Miller taught lessons to the community where she resided and also operated a kindergarten catering to African- American children in Inman, South Carolina, in the 1970s.

Toni was the middle child of three and grew up in Spartanburg in the 1970s and 1980s with her older sister, Sonya, and younger brother, Trey (Raymond III). Their parents were high school teachers and stressed church, education, music/fine arts, and ambition in raising all their children. Their mother, Mary (Ferguson) Arnold, an accomplished musician, was a part of the large Ferguson family, known in the local area for their singing and playing abilities. Mary was a church musician and private piano instructor in the community. She and her sisters also sang in a gospel group called the Ferguson Sisters in the late 1950s to early 1970s. There were ten children in Mary's family. All four girls and two of her brothers were also excellent vocalists or musicians. In 1979 she passed away at the age of 42 from cancer, yet their father, Raymond Arnold Jr., continued to raise the three children as a single father with the help and love of family and friends in the community.

Raymond, who still resides in Spartanburg, was a jack of all trades, including skillfulness in carpentry, woodworking, automotive mechanics, and vehicle sales. He owned and operated a soul food restaurant, owned and managed rental properties, owned a record store, and did small- scale farming. He also was involved in NASCAR in the 1960s and1970s on the first African-American racing team, #34, of the late Wendell Scott. He played drums, sang in local bands, performed as a local disc jockey during that same time, and was an old-school party DJ. He was a musical enthusiast and maintained an extensive collection of R&B, soul, funk, and gospel music and civil rights sermons from that time period. The musical abilities of both parents inspired Sonya to be an accomplished classical violinist and Trey to be an accomplished violin bassist, jazz drummer, and DJ. All three children were formally trained in school district 7 of Spartanburg and studied privately as well. All three children continued a connection to music after graduating from college and into their adulthood.

Toni studied first under her mom from the ages of four to six and then attended the Yamaha School of Music in Spartanburg for several years. She studied classical piano for eight years from ages nine to seventeen in the Converse Pre-College Music Program in her hometown. Toni also played violin during those years and participated in the school orchestra. At 14, she played at her home church, Upper Shady Grove Missionary Baptist, in Wellford. She sang and played in teenage choirs and coordinated music for the Black History Gospel Choir at Spartanburg Senior High School. In her teenage years in the late 1980s, she became a part of the local music scene by participating as a keyboardist for various hip-hop, R&B, and gospel ensembles. This included recording keys on several songs that obtained local radio airplay. She did some co-writing of music and openings for national acts at the local arena. Exploring songwriting further, she submitted various compositions to music contests. She placed third in a high school state level music contest with her first copyrighted gospel composition, "Dear God." During this time she also studied classical violin for eight years while continuing to study piano. With the help of several music colleagues and instructor Dr. Sheri Mitchell, she held her own senior recital at age 17 at Converse College. Her recital included various classical compositions and popular music. Toni moved to Raleigh in 1987 to attend North Carolina State University, where she continued to join various local bands, sang in the college gospel choir, New Horizons, and eventually became a church musician. While in college she worked part time in urban services at the Central Branch YMCA. While there, she worked with a choir of at-risk youth, eventually renaming the choir New Images. She composed and copyrighted a touching theme song, also called "New Images," that brought the choir much publicity as they performed it for area fundraising campaigns.

In 1996, already employed as a full-time engineer, Toni graduated from North Carolina State University with a B.S in mechanical engineering and a minor in African-American studies. While there, she sang with the highly acclaimed New Horizons Choir. She remained in Raleigh after graduation and joined the corporate world in engineering. In the evenings and on weekends, her passion for music continued to be very much alive. She played keyboards for a local R&B group called II Sharp and eventually focused her passion on gospel music by serving at local churches. She returned to school as a mid-career engineer to earn a master of business administration degree from the University of Phoenix in 2007. Additionally, she obtained internationally recognized technical certification in the field of quality as a Certified Six Sigma Black Belt in 2008 as a part of her employment for John Deere. This allowed her to provide technical expertise to project management and improvement of quality in products and processes.

Toni will leverage her corporate and musical skill sets, along with her doctor of ministry degree in creative arts from the Graduate Theological Foundation of Mishawaka, Indiana. Her concentration is on the evolution of African-American worship, from music ministry to music industry, as pursued by the independent gospel artist. As a part of her doctoral research, she launched an initiative called Gospel Music One Sound to investigate the current-day landscape of gospel music in the local church, the community, and the music industry. The research included a symposium and concert, headlining national gospel artist William Becton, whom she had understudied musically and spiritually since 2006. She will continue to package this research as seminars, webinars, books, and certifications to help streamline the journey of the gospel artist from ministry to industry. Her aim is to unify and renew the purpose of gospel music practitioners who labor in church and in the gospel music industry. The name "Gospel

Music One Sound" was revealed to Toni during the doctoral research and was inspired by reading 2 Chronicles 5:13 as the measure of effectiveness in worship. In this scripture when the musicians and vocalists praised the Lord and gave Him thanks in unison, in one accord, a thick cloud, which was the glory of the Lord, filled the temple. She sees this as the goal for the ultimate Christian worship arts worldwide, with her specialty on the effectiveness of the African-American worship landscape. Gospel Music One Sound will seek best techniques to guide the church music ministry leader and gospel artist. The gospel artist and church music ministry leader have an opportunity to work together to leverage three platforms (the local church, the community, and the music industry marketplace) for kingdom building. Toni's anticipated graduation is May 2016.

Toni is married to Tony D. McFarland Sr., an accomplished lead guitarist from the gospel venue in the Raleigh area. Tony has an extensive musical bio that stems from his childhood and a group with his brothers called Lights of Joy in Raleigh. In his adult years he recorded with a quartet group called the Goldenaires and a new traditional group called Encovenant.

They both have served in the music ministry at Oak City Baptist Church in Raleigh, where she was music director. Shortly after their marriage in 2005, they founded a gospel ensemble called Blessed Union, The Group, which is pursuing the gospel music industry. The talented ensemble has worked with various national artists in stage productions and is mentored by national recording artist William Becton. In January 2014, they performed at the New Artist Showcase held at the Stellar Awards Weekend in Nashville. In the spring of 2015, the group released two digital downloads written by Toni called "I'm Covered" and "Your Love Is All I Need." These are available for purchase on I-Tunes, Amazon, Google Play, and CD Baby marketplaces. They can be heard by live streaming on YouTube and Spotify. Visit blessedunion.org for further details and booking information.

THE VISION

As a couple in ministry, Toni and Tony enjoy being able to share their divine connection in music to grow together, enhance music ministries, and develop others. They understand the healing and transformational power that music can have when anointing is able to leverage a compassionate heart and technical skill. Their vision for music ministry is modeled on the Levites. In 1 Chronicles 15:22, Kenaniah is in charge of singing based on his skill, and in 1 Chronicles 25:7, Levites were all trained and skilled in the music of the Lord.

CHAPTER 1
Introduction

The purpose of this research is to focus on the evolution of the African-American Christian's worship experience and worship space and the changing facets of black sacred music that led to gospel music as ministry in the mainstream music industry. The African-American worship experience has evolved since the first Africans arrived in North America in 1619. Remnants of African spirituality, such as the ring shout and spirit possession, survived the horrors of slavery and are still recognizably influential in African-American worship. In African-American worship today there exists a unity in diversity that transcends denomination and even faiths. The expressions of music, dance, song, oratorical preaching style, and call and response with the congregation are all key characteristics of the African-American church (Hayes, 2002).

The value of this research is that it provides an analytical review of how the current-day role and responsibilities of gospel music ministry practitioners of the church, community, and gospel music industry can realize an opportunity in ministry growth and expansion. This occurs by achieving commercial gain and sustainability from leveraging secular practices and influences. These practitioners include roles as musician, worship leader, preacher, vocalist in the gospel choir, ensembles, and exalters of the church. This can also occur at the local, regional, national, and international levels in worship space, music venues, and ministry venues via media and entertainment venues of all sizes.

Slaves began establishing worship space on the plantation in secret places known as "brush or hush arbor." A key contributor of the experience was the exalter, often a preacher/singer who would lead the slaves in call and response cadences (Hayes, 2002). The music was provided with the voice and body as the instrument. Drums eventually were forbidden, as they carried the beats brought through the slave trade. A trace of the African-American history timeline and social movement parallels the evolution of this initially volunteer role, eventually being split between the preacher and choir director or musician. It eventually evolved to a paid role in the African-American church following the paid role of the pastor. Over time, the opportunities for the musician/singer groomed in the church transcended beyond the four walls of the church and birthed a new platform in ministry. The gospel music artist is now able to secure a competitive position in the music industry market place. This is far beyond the vision of the early role of the slave ship song leader and the brush arbor preacher/singer/exalter.

This research addresses the needs of the independent gospel music artist who is challenged to maintain substance and Christian relevance amidst the competing agenda of the overall music industry. The scope of this research, as mentioned earlier, is African-American Christian worship. The focus is on the exalter, in today's time most closely resembling the gospel music artist. This can be an individual or a group of individuals who exalt the gospel of Christ through music.

The literature review begins with the slavery era up through post-reconstruction in order to lay the historical foundation of black sacred music prior to the birth of gospel. The primary timeline of this research is from the birth of gospel music in the early 1930s, promoted by Thomas A Dorsey, who is known as the father of gospel music, up to the entrance of Kirk Franklin in the early 1990s and the continuation of Franklin and other key influences from 2000 until 2015. Dorsey's contributions revolutionized the genre and introduced an urban style that continues to evolve. Dorsey wrote "Precious Lord, Take My Hand" upon receiving the news of the death of his wife and son in August 1932. The birth that occurred out of this pain would change the African-American worship experience. It was the seed planted for gospel music at this moment that fused blues chords from secular music with sacred lyrics crying out to the Lord (Public Broadcast System, 2003). This style was a trend that evolved for approximately 30 years until the baton was passed to James Cleveland in the 1960s, whose work with recording and developing mass choirs made him the king of gospel. Cleveland had been a singer at Mt. Pilgrim Baptist Church, where Thomas Dorsey was the minister of music. Cleveland was followed by contemporary influences of Andraé Crouch and Edwin and Walter Hawkins, who transitioned the sound of gospel music from traditional to contemporary style.

One could argue that it was divine intervention when James Cleveland died in 1991, six months after Kirk Franklin directed the mass choir at his brain child organization, GMWA. Two years later, Dorsey passed away in 1993, just after Kirk Franklin entered the national music scene in 1992. Franklin's series of CD hits like *Stomp* and groups he produced brought a new expectation, standard, and style that urbanized gospel and crossed genres and cultures, revolutionizing gospel music (All Music, 2015)

A close look at this era will demonstrate how it has evolved from "worship-service-only" music to a multifaceted style that generates revenue for the overall music and entertainment industry. For practical purposes this work focuses on solutions and recommendations for the independent gospel artist who is not signed to a major label. Many of them start their own labels or at one time were on major labels. These artists have flexibility in ways major label artists may not. This may sound appealing, yet it requires the artist to manage all key contributing factors to his or her success that would normally be handled by the resources of a major record label. All music artists, of all genres, at some point may be challenged to compromise personal beliefs and values in exchange for opportunities in the industry. This is even more challenging for gospel artists because their music and image are supposed to represent biblical values and the message of Christ. If the music sounds too much like "worldly" music, or if the artist's appearance and style are too much like secular artists, he or she can become ostracized and considered insincere and too edgy. The artist may even become an outcast of the African-American church community. The timeline of gospel music demonstrates how this conflict about what is considered "acceptable" has evolved over time. The gospel music of today must now compete with mainstream music, and success is measured by business metrics, such as record sales, peak charting position on Billboard, and performance on Nielsen ratings. Artists, regardless of genre, gain more control of their destiny once they are proven; however, they must continue to stay competitive in the marketplace to sustain popularity and to maintain their platform for the Christian message.

Problem Statement and Hypothesis

Herein lies the problem: the independent gospel artist is challenged to balance ministry against the demands of the music industry. As a disciple of Christ, the independent gospel artist is expected to spread the gospel through song while not compromising or conforming to the conflicting values of the music industry aimed at mainstream cultural appeal. In other words, how do independent gospel artists balance ministry focus against the demands of the industry and sustain effectiveness without compromising their Christian faith?

The answer lies in the research that traces the history and evolution of gospel music and in the various participants and factors that enable it. This approach arrives at best practices, trends of influential artists, industry professionals, and local church/community music ministry leaders in current times. When these elements are coupled with supportive changes in social acceptance, attitude, or perception, the environment for transformation and possibilities is fertilized. Thus, sustainable and effective improvements can take root.

As a hypothesis, the history of gospel music demonstrates continuity in the elements of gospel music with necessary adaptations, in an accepted form, from the Dorsey to the Franklin era. As gospel music evolves, so has the social acceptance of what was once controversial in art form, practices, and venue. This has liberated the next generation of gospel artists to have greater opportunity for ministry while leveraging the music industry.

Constraints and Limitations

One constraint of this research was that there is no single authority or resource on the evolution of African-American worship and the development of gospel music. Various works from different scholarly sources had to be compiled to obtain the complete story, and there were some minor differences in interpretation and documentation of findings. A good portion of the content had to be obtained ethnographically. One limitation in the research was in determining a tangible measure of the effectiveness of the ministry of the gospel artist. Research compiled looked at qualitative findings on ministry contributions to measure ministry effectiveness.

Definitions

The following primary definitions of this work provide knowledge leveling on the primary topic. The following review of these key definitions sets the angle and point of view for discussion and understanding.

What is gospel music? It is a music based on Christian doctrine and ideals, telling of the good news and testimony, and was popularized in the African-American tradition. It consists of distinct biblical themes, vocals, instrumentation characteristics, and movement, such as foot stomping, hand clapping, vocal shouting and embellishing, dancing, and other physical demonstrations as an outcome of heartfelt emotion and encounters with the Holy Spirit. Instrumentation generally includes at a minimum piano, organ, and other keyboard sounds. Over time it has evolved often to include drums, percussion, bass guitar, lead guitar, horn instruments, and synthesized sounds. Delivery of music began as spirit-filled, soul-stirring exaltations that have evolved since its first recognition in the 1920s. Earlier forms and predecessors of gospel music include Negro spirituals, black folk church songs, lined hymns, Black Church hymnody, sacred songs/anthems, shaped note songs, devotional/congregational songs, and songs sung by soloists, ensembles, choirs, quartet singers, shape note singers, congregations, communal singers and/or exalters in call and response style. Current sub-genres and designations of gospel music include but are not limited to urban gospel, R&B gospel, R&P (rhythm and praise), Christian hip-hop, traditional (black) gospel, new traditional gospel, contemporary gospel, modern Christian, Christian contemporary, quartet music, inspirational music, gospel/inspirational jazz, neo-soul, and praise and worship. Gospel music has had strong influences on other music genres such as soul and rock and roll. This definition was developed by personal and field experience, from research, and from a combination of resources including Dicitonary.com (2015), interviews with black sacred music scholar Professor L. Stanley Davis (2015), and content in *The Gospel Music Industry Round-Up* by Lisa Collins (2015).

What is a gospel artist? This is the soloist, choir, or group who performs gospel music (as described in the definition) in pursuit of a sustainable ministry and business position in the gospel music industry.

What is the gospel music industry? This is a segment of the larger music industry. It is a segment of the Christian music industry that focuses on commercial level production, distribution and sale of music and related products, services, events, and performances. The research focuses on gospel music that appeals to African-American culture.

What is African-American worship? First, one must understand what *worship* is. As defined by Webster's dictionary, it is reverence offered a divine being or supernatural power; also an act of expressing such reverence. In the context of this work, African-American worship is worship influenced by the social and cultural experiences of African-Americans. The scope of this work is on African-American Christian worship. The worship space goes beyond the four walls of the church. The gospel artist and others recognized as key figures in Christianity are able to be a part of mainstream popular culture on television, in movies, via print and online media, and in the music and entertainment industry. This occurs at the risk of commercialization, which can dilute authenticity.

According to African-American music and worship scholar Melva Wilson Consten, the worship of African-American Christians is influenced by at least four streams of tradition: traditional African primal world views; Judeo-Christian religion; African-American folk religion, which emanated from worldviews shaped in the American context in a crisis of slavery and oppression; and Western/Euro-American Christianity. She further explains African-American leitourgia (liturgy) as the work of the people as ritual action, ministry, and service. It is reflective of the experiences of a particular people deeply aware of the power and promise of God. The definition of African-American worship will be further synthesized in the body of this work.

What is the Black Church? A discussion on music of the African-American church tradition and worship experience must begin with a foundational understanding of the Black Church (the African-American church) and how important it is to African-Americans. It is important for current day practitioners of gospel music to understand the history of the Black Church, the denominations and belief systems, and the worship experience in the difference settings.

The term *the Black Church* must not be misinterpreted as a monolithic description of African-American Christianity. According to the PBS documentary *God in America: The Black Church*, this term evolved from the term *the Negro church*, W. E. B. Dubois's pioneering research project on African-American Protestants. This academic study was completed at the turn of the century and revealed the diversity and decentralization of African-American Protestant faith. Scholars, including those in the documentary *God in America: The Black Church* and *The African-American Heritage Hymnal*, have noted that the term *the Black Church* today includes the seven major historically black denominations with which 80% of black Christians are affiliated:

- African Methodist Episcopal Church (A.M.E.)
- African Methodist Episcopal Zion Church (A.M.E.Z.)
- Christian Methodist Episcopal (C.M.E, formerly Colored Methodist Episcopal)
- The National Baptist Convention, U.S.A., Incorporated (N.B.C)
- The National Baptist Convention of America, Unincorporated (N.B.C.A.)

- The Progressive National Baptist Convention (P.N.B.C.)
- The Church of God in Christ (C.O.G.I.C.)

The African-American registry website (2013) views the Black Church as the savior of oppressed African people in the United States of America. Throughout African-American history, it has been the center of black life. The Black Church has been an incubator for social change and has influenced cultural developments, arts, music, education, social views, and political views since African slaves began independent worship without their slave masters. The Black Church has birthed and mothered impactful social activists, preachers, politicians, educators, inventors, lawyers, athletes, entertainers, and other contributors to society who have helped improve the quality of life against the odds of oppression for African-Americans. These types of individuals, with strong commitment to their faith and in some instances transcending into non-Christian religion, are known in every African-American community at local, regional, national, and international levels for their impact and strides of progress.

The main entities of worship service in the Black Church include the sermon, usually delivered by the pastor or another preacher; the music, primarily led by the choir or identified singers; and the response to these by the congregation. These three groups of participants can "have church" at any place and at any time. The term to "have church" is commonly used in the Black Church in reference to having an elated worship experience that lifts emotional burdens when all these entities interact effectively. The worship experience does not necessarily have to be in an edifice called "the church." As history reveals, enslaved Africans began having church even as they lay on their backs shackled like animals on slave ships. From their different religious backgrounds and languages, they found a spirituality that connected them to have call-and-response singing while a natural-born leader might exalt an encoded escape method and strategy to take over the ship. Once in the new land, slaves would sneak away to brush arbors, often called "hush harbors," to have church in their own way, with the emotional fervor and freedom they knew in Africa. This was the alternative to being spectators in the church services some were allowed to attend with their masters, sitting at the back or in galleries. White slave masters felt a need to oversee African-American worship in fear of insurrection and used these services as a means for biblically justifying bondage.

Early churches established by slaves became the catalyst for social change, and the role of the black preacher was at the forefront. Black ministers risked their lives and were often arrested and beaten for organizing slaves to establish their own churches. The African-American registry records the first known slave congregation established on the William Byrd III Plantation in Mecklenburg County, Virginia, in 1758, before the American Revolution. One of the early recorded black churches, the African Baptist Church, established in 1777 in Savannah, Georgia, was established with the help of Minister George Leile. Philadelphia became a hub and haven for free blacks and fugitive slaves. Richard Allen, a former slave who had purchased his freedom, and Absalom Jones were the leaders of the Free African Society, established in 1787. These two preacher activists used this organization to mobilize the movement of black churches in other cities and would become pivotal founding fathers in African-American history. Richard Allen led the establishment of Bethel African Methodist Episcopal Church in 1794 after purchasing land, building the edifice, and receiving the dedication by the predominantly white Methodist Episcopal Church. This church is the oldest parcel of real estate in the United States owned continuously by African-Americans. Allen would later be ordained in 1799 as the first black minister in the Methodist denomination. His colleague in abolishing slavery, Absalom Jones, would eventually become the first black priest ordained in the Episcopal Church in the United States in 1804. Additionally, Allen and his wife, Sara Bass Allen, utilized the church to support the Underground Railroad, as did other black and white abolitionists, many of them also ministers (*The African-American Registry*, 2013).

During the post-Civil War era, newly freed blacks were eager to establish their own churches. The black ministers of the South continued to take the charge that led to the formation of these independently operating black congregations, many of them in the Baptist denomination. A former slave from South Carolina, Rev. Alexander Bettis, established more than 40 churches in the South from 1865 to 1895 (*The African-American Registry*, 2013).

The litany of involvement of the black minister continued to set the vision of the black community, while the church often served as a school, community center, and town hall meeting place. This momentum set by the early black ministers continued up through the Jim Crow laws and civil rights era, with a host of advocacy for social change, ultimately led by Dr. Martin Luther King Jr. He mobilized numerous black pastors and their congregations as a network for participation in non-violent protests for social equality. White clergy also became involved and participated in the movement. The Black Church, under the leadership of black clergy, has been the backbone of African-American history and continues to play a significant role today.

A data-demonstrated analysis of the importance of faith, which includes the Black Church, was revealed by the 2008 Pew Religious Landscape Survey. The results display that African-Americans are more likely than any other racial group to report a formal religious affiliation. Additionally, even those who consider themselves unaffiliated describe their religious status as *religiously* unaffiliated. The results indicate that 87% of African-Americans consider themselves a part of a religious group, compared with 83% of the public overall. The study shows that 79% of African-Americans reported religion as very important in their lives, which is more than the 56% of all U.S. adults.

Fifty-nine percent (59%) of African-Americans belong to historically black Protestant denominations (referred to as the Black Church), 15% belong to evangelical Protestant denominations, 4% to the mainline protest, 5% to Catholic. Twelve percent (12%) listed themselves as unaffiliated, 5% as other (including Muslims, Jews, Buddhists, Hindus), and 1% as unknown or "refused to answer."

Interestingly, of the 12% of unaffiliated African-Americans, only 1% considered themselves atheist or agnostic. The remaining 11% said they were not affiliated with a particular religion yet still had religious beliefs. Seventy-two percent (72%) of the unaffiliated still viewed religion as somewhat important, and 45% still viewed it as very important.

The study also looked at religious practices such as frequency of prayer, attendance of services, and absolute certainty that God exists. It revealed that 70% of the unaffiliated African-Americans voiced absolute certainty that God exists and were comparable to the 73% of mainline Protestant (US overall) and 70% of Catholics (US overall). The study noted that 88% of African-Americans overall have absolute certainty that God exists.

Overall, African-Americans are 78% Protestant, compared with 51% of the U.S. adult population. These results align to the historical trace of Protestant influence in African-American history. The survey revealed that African-Americans demonstrate being the most religious ethnic group in the United States in regard to certainty of belief in God, frequency of prayer, frequency of church attendance, and importance of religion.

CHAPTER 2

Theological Framework

To explore the topic of gospel music ministry versus music industry, a theological framework must be established to guide the development of the discussion, the explanation of content, and the way it is applied to the topic. The content of this research will be discussed within the context of the theological framework.

The driving force and motivation of the argument is centered on one's perception of worship. Opinions vary about the definition of true and authentic worship, which is the key ingredient in music ministry. When popular culture influences the practices in the church, especially in worship arts like music, Christians often lean to the following scripture for theological support for not looking like the world:

> And do not be conformed to this world, but be transformed by the renewing of your mind, that you may prove what is that good and acceptable and perfect will of God.
> – Romans 12:2 NKJV

This conflict of interest faced by the gospel artist brings into question the motivation and authenticity of his or her worship of God. In other words, as Christians, adherence or conformance to His perfect will, which is defined by the Word of God, is a measure of how well we worship Him. The decisions we set our minds to should be acceptable in His eyes and not conform to the world. Before we can examine the conformance of the demonstration of worship by the gospel artist to the theology of worship in the Holy Bible, we must first define *worship* and establish an understanding of worship from applicable perspectives.

The answers to the following questions form the basic foundations of the theological framework of this research. These answers are based on scholars of worship, specifically of African-American worship, and on the Holy Bible. These resources aid in the understanding of the debate on the responsibility of the gospel artist in the African-American Christian worship space. This space has evolved over time. It went from the African village, slave ships, plantation brush harbors, and private homes and property to early African-American churches of the twentieth century, and eventually to concert halls, auditoriums, radio, TV, and now other forms of 21st-century mainstream media and venues in the music and entertainment industry.

1) What is the basic definition of worship?
2) What is the theological definition of worship?
3) What is the biblical definition of worship?
4) What is the theological framework of worship in the African-American church?

Continued discussion of each of these questions will occur at various points throughout this exposition as the analysis unfolds. Taking this approach enables critical thinking on the definition of worship and how it has evolved in the African-American cultural context.

What Is the Basic Definition of Worship?

For this study it is important to have a clear understanding of what worship is. *Merriam Webster* provides two perspectives of the definitions. The first definition is from a spiritual view, and the second is from a secular view. These represent what society views as worship.

1) reverence offered a divine being or supernatural power; an act of expressing such reverence; a form of religious practice with its creed and ritual
2) extravagant respect or admiration for or devotion to an object of esteem; synonymous to idolatry

What Is the Theological Definition of Worship?

Next, one must understand the theological definition of worship that bridges the basic definition to biblical worship. The theological definition of worship for this research will be examined from two perspectives: 1) the individual worshiper and 2) the corporate and unified worship of believers. An exploration of the theologies of worship presented by Harold M. Best in *Unceasing Worship: Biblical Perspectives on Worship and the Arts* as well as theologies presented by Robert E. Webber in his seven-volume *The Complete Library of Christian Worship* will aid in this. Best fits into the field of systematic theology and Webber's works fit into worship theology. Best (2003) provides an analysis of worship from the perspective of the individual worshiper while Webber's analysis of the Bible focuses on corporate worship as a formal and professional expression.

Best recognizes the difference between the secular/worldly and spiritual views of worship. For the individual worshiper, Harold Best in chapter 1 of *Unceasing Worship* defines worship as the continuous outpouring of "all that I am, all that I do and all that I can ever become" in light of a god already chosen or being chosen. First, the definition covers all mankind and does not focus just on Christians. It covers the submission of people everywhere and their submission to whatever masters them and their witness as to why they live the way they do. The gods of the human race are not necessarily God.

In society we place emphasis on worship at specific times and places and on methods used. As a result, Best states, there are misunderstandings of the biblical meaning of worship. It is interesting how he explains that worship may ebb and flow and take on various appearances. It can be conscious or unconscious, intense, ecstatic, quiet, or commonplace. Nonetheless, it will always be continuous. Sin does not stop worship. It causes worship to change directions to perhaps something that is detrimental or not good for us, even if only for an instant. We get distracted, and the only solution is repentance. In a general sense, repentance is turning from what is not good for us and turning back to what is good for us (Best, 2003).

The gospel artist is challenged to keep worship continuous while operating in the temptations of the gospel music industry, which is a sub-genre of the music industry. Business partners and executives focus on business metrics that may not align with God's plans and Christian teachings.

What Is the Biblical Definition of Worship?

Best transitions to provide a biblical view of worship for the individual worshiper. It is called *authentic worship* and begins by expressing how Christ the Savior has come. Christ has come to man from the eternities, and because He has come, man's outpouring no longer needs to be wasted being lost in secular worship and idolizing false gods. Continuous outpouring can be made pure again. Best states that authentic worship can be only in Christ and is not driven by a liturgy, call to worship, or change in style. Redemption and worship become one, and the original plan for Eden is restored and surpassed. The desired outcome and ultimate goal for Christians is to worship God in an acceptable manner that yields redemption and restoration. The challenge to Christians is to pursue this acceptance of holiness while living among the temptations on earth that yield sin. The sins are distracters from authentic and true worship to God (Best, 2003).

To explain continuous outpouring and its relation to spirit and truth, Best focuses on salvation and authentic worship in John 4. He notes that the Samaritan woman saw worship as an occasion, as a time, place, or tradition, while Christ unified salvation and authentic worship. Jesus prepared the way for Romans 12–16, and His response illustrated that true worship is continuous while time and location are incidental. Salvation and authentic worship together mean always being in Spirit and in truth.

For today's Christian, this means Spirit and truth are to be manifested in the workplace, home, and school the same way they are displayed in the corporate assemblies. This worship looks beyond liturgies and methodologies. When believers depend primarily on liturgies, dances, songs, and other traditional aspects of worship, they violate the principles of faith, hope, love, spirit, and truth and the reality of sacrificial living (Best, 2003).

The study will look at challenges the gospel artist faces when worship occurs in non-church settings. Based on this interpretation from Best, the gospel artist is freed up to worship anywhere if it is in Spirit and in truth and aligns with sacrificial living.

Webber's Perspective on Corporate Worship

Webber's focus on worship provides the corporate worship perspective and the role of music in aiding believers to experience God. This examination of music in worship exemplified in the Bible assists in the development of the theological framework. Robert E. Webber's *The Complete Library of Christian Worship (A Brief History of Music in Worship)* provides a synopsis of music in the worship of the Old and New Testaments.

He notes the Old Testament Jewish synagogue worship and modern Christian services are similar in content and spirit, and music has been inseparable from worship in both instances. Psalms represent early heritage worship songs and periods of ancient Jewish culture. Synagogue music had cantors/soloists who were possibly trained in the temple Levitical ministry. There was some congregation involvement. Moses and his sister, the prophetess Miriam, are accredited with the first musical reference in the Bible. They sang thanksgiving when God delivered the Israelites from the Egyptians. Miriam played a tambourine and sang, "I will sing to the Lord, For He has triumphed gloriously! The horse and its rider He has thrown into the sea!" (Exodus 15:1). As she sang and danced, other ladies followed. This expression of praise is an example of how others worshiped in the Old Testament, specifically in the book of Psalms. Webber refers to two musical traditions in the Old Testament mentioned by Erik Routley. First, they were spontaneous and ecstatic, and second, they were formal and professional. *Spontaneous and ecstatic worship* is found in the scriptural references below. This passage refers to the time when Saul was preparing to become king of Israel and the prophet Samuel provided instructions.

> After that you shall come to the hill of God where the Philistine garrison *is*. And it will happen, when you have come there to the city that you will meet a group of prophets coming down from the high place with a stringed instrument, a tambourine, a flute, and a harp before them; and they will be prophesying. Then the Spirit of the Lord will come upon you, and you will prophesy with them and be turned into another man.
> —1 Samuel 10:5–6 NKJV

Second Kings 3:15–16 refers to the time when the prophet Elisha foretold God's judgment. Music assisted in the worshipers' experience of God.

> "But now bring me a musician."
>
> Then it happened, when the musician played, that the hand of the Lord came upon him. And he said, "Thus says the Lord: 'Make this valley full of ditches.'"
> —2 Kings 3:15–16 NKJV

Examples of the *formal and professional* exhibit of music in worship in the Old Testament are found in 1 Chronicles when the ark of God was being moved to Jerusalem and in the book of Psalms.

These examples of music in the temple were initiated by King David, well known for his skillful music abilities as a harpist and hymn composer.

> Then David spoke to the leaders of the Levites to appoint their brethren to be the singers accompanied by instruments of music, stringed instruments, harps, and cymbals, by raising the voice with resounding joy. . . . Chenaniah, leader of the Levites, was instructor in charge of the music, because he was skillful. . . . David was clothed with a robe of fine linen, as were all the Levites who bore the ark, the singers, and Chenaniah the music master with the singers. David also wore a linen ephod. Thus all Israel brought up the ark of the covenant of the Lord with shouting and with the sound of the horn, with trumpets and with cymbals, making music with stringed instruments and harps.
> —1 Chronicles 15:16, 22, 27–28 NKJV

Psalm 150 displays the musical instrumentation found in ancient Hebrew worship. Webber notes that in ancient Hebrew worship, the words of Scripture were never to be spoken without melody, as this would be considered inappropriate. Scripture was always sung in fervent cantillation and accompanied by instruments, which provided embellishment to the vocal melody. Psalm 150 shows an example of how dance is included in ancient Hebrew worship. This is a well-known reference in scripture in African-American worship, as it demonstrates the celebrative praise akin to African-American heritage.

> Praise the Lord!
> Praise God in His sanctuary;
> Praise Him in His mighty firmament!
>
> Praise Him for His mighty acts;
> Praise Him according to His excellent greatness!

Praise Him with the sound of the trumpet;
Praise Him with the lute and harp!
Praise Him with the timbrel and dance;
Praise Him with stringed instruments and flutes!
Praise Him with loud cymbals;
Praise Him with clashing cymbals!
Let everything that has breath praise the Lord.
Praise the Lord!

—Psalm 150 NKJV

An example of how unified singing and instrumentation in the formal and professional setting is significant in experiencing God in worship is found at the dedication of Solomon's temple. In 2 Chronicles 5:11–14, God was so pleased that He revealed His presence through the musical performance.

> And it came to pass when the priests came out of the Most Holy Place (for all the priests who were present had sanctified themselves, without keeping to their divisions), and the Levites who were the singers, all those of Asaph and Heman and Jeduthun, with their sons and their brethren, stood at the east end of the altar, clothed in white linen, having cymbals, stringed instruments and harps, and with them one hundred and twenty priests sounding with trumpets—indeed it came to pass, when the trumpeters and singers were as one, to make one sound to be heard in praising and thanking the Lord, and when they lifted up their voice with the trumpets and cymbals and instruments of music, and praised the Lord, saying:
>
> "For He is good,
> For His mercy endures forever,"
>
> that the house, the house of the Lord, was filled with a cloud, so that the priests could not continue ministering because of the cloud; for the glory of the Lord filled the house of God.
>
> –2 Chronicles 5:11–14 NKJV

In the New Testament, music is not mentioned as extensively as in the Old Testament. As Webber points out in his assessment of the music in the New Testament from the *Worship Library*, most of the references are conceptual rather than literal. The instructions for music are found mainly in the epistles, most of them given by Paul. A demonstration of music as a tool for worship in the New Testament is found in Paul's instructions in the following passage:

> Therefore let him who speaks in a tongue pray that he may interpret. For if I pray in a tongue, my spirit prays, but my understanding is unfruitful. What is the conclusion then? I will pray with the spirit, and I will also pray with the understanding. I will sing with the spirit, and I will also sing with the understanding.
>
> How is it then, brethren? Whenever you come together, each of you has a psalm, has a teaching, has a tongue, has a revelation, has an interpretation. Let all things be done for edification.
>
> –1 Corinthians 14:13–15, 26 NKJV

Webber explains that Paul is calling for a balance between ecstasy and discipline in music making (as well as praying) by asking that singing be done with the mind (or understanding) as well as in the spirit. He advises that singing (as well as teaching, revelations, and speaking in tongues) be done for edification along with all things. Other well-known passages instructing on how music is to be executed among believers are included in the following scriptures from Ephesians and Colossians:

> Speaking to one another in psalms and hymns and spiritual songs, singing and making melody in your heart to the Lord.
>
> –Ephesians 5:19 NKJV

> Let the word of Christ dwell in you richly in all wisdom, teaching and admonishing one another in psalms and hymns and spiritual songs, singing with grace in your hearts to the Lord. And whatever you do in word or deed, do all in the name of the Lord Jesus, giving thanks to God the Father through Him.
>
> – Colossians 3:16–17 NKJV

Webber brings to light a philosophy on music of the New Testament that the use of music in worship is exceedingly broad. He states that what the New Testament leaves unsaid about music is a healthy quality. Webber girds this understanding in the following scripture:

> I know and am convinced by the Lord Jesus that there is nothing unclean of itself; but to him who considers anything to be unclean, to him it is unclean.
>
> –Romans 14:14 NKJV

Webber states that the distinction, therefore, between the pagan concept of the empowerment of things and the Christian concept of discernment among things, none of which are impure in themselves or empowered, overrides any opinion that states that the early church set a standard in music that was rigid, unchangeable, and limited. Webber concludes that the range of musical practice in the New Testament is rather to be construed as broadly as possible because it is based on a principle that speaks to a total way of life, including music.

These concepts reviewed by Webber apply to the thesis research in several ways. As the literature review will reveal, a dichotomy in African-American worship styles unveiled in the early developments of African-American worship set the boundaries for denominational styles; the ecstatic style was more favored by the Pentecostal congregations and the formal and professional style of the Protestant churches influenced by European worship. The black sacred music that evolves from spirituals to gospel music flows more closely with the ecstatic style. His assessment of the New Testament's take on musical practices as a part of a total way of life can be viewed as a "liberating" perspective on how gospel music should go beyond the four walls of the church. This includes going into untapped aspects of life such as TV, radio, and leisure listening.

What Is the Theological Framework of Worship in the African-American Church?

An in-depth understanding of African-American spirituality and its role in ministry provides an understanding of the theological framework of worship in the African-American church. This independent study covered African-American spirituality, its impact upon the development of sacred music (from the spirituals through contemporary gospel music) in African-American church traditions, and the role that African-American sacred music, as an aspect of African-American spirituality, plays in churches today.

A compilation of the key learning themes, objectives, and take-away items on material by scholars in African-American spirituality is presented in Appendix 2 Table 17. This overview aids in understanding the theological framework of worship in the African-American church. These works include 1) *Forged in the Fiery Furnace—African-American Spirituality,* by Diana Hayes, 2) *Deep River and the Negro Spiritual Speaks of Life and Death,* by Howard Thurman, and 3) *The Spirituals and the Blues,* by James Cone.

In *Forged in the Fiery Furnace-African-American Spirituality,* the author intricately dissects the historical development of African spirituality and its evolving to African-American spirituality. Hayes also explains the past and present theologies of the emerging Black Church. In *Deep River,* Thurman dissects the lyrics of Negro spirituals and interprets how they provide insight to life as a slave. Thurman delivered *The Negro Spiritual Speaks of Life and Death* for the Ingersoll Lecture on Immortality of Man at Harvard Divinity School. In *The Spirituals and the Blues,* Thurman interprets how Negro spirituals reflect on life and death. Cone's advocacy of black liberation theology and his alignment to Malcom X is evident in his interpretations. The primary theme of this text is that the spirituals and the blues are about the power of song in the struggle for black survival. He discusses how the blues reflect a non-spiritual response to the day-to-day struggles of being black in America.

Concepts from Diana Hayes

Diana Hayes's approach to dissecting the content helps the reader understand African spirituality through the eyes of Western Christianity. In order to understand African-American spirituality, one must first understand the ingredients that create the unique flavor of this ethnic group. She states that what African-Americans have been taught about African religion has been influenced by European understanding of African religion. A system intended to enslave Africans living in a strange land is the fiery furnace that births a strong faith that will become foundational in American history and in the fabric of American culture. Africans brought Ntu with them to America. This is a key distinction in today's African-American worship as spiritual encounters. It is the spiritual life force from our African origins that connects us with ancestors and is incorporated in the Christianity of the slaves. African-American Christians have continued to hold strong to distinct traits of our spirituality. The result is the cultural divide that exists every Sunday morning at 11 o'clock, known as the most segregated hour in America (2002).

As the early Black Church emerged, so did social justice and contemporary witness. The secret worship that evolved to independent structured institutions survived slavery and was the pillar of strength during the post-reconstruction years. A major theology that emerged during this era was a spirituality that became the basis for ethical leadership and social transformation. In the text, Hayes reviews various spiritualties, including spirituality of a people, soul survivors, combative spirituality, pragmatic spirituality, and alternative spiritualties. She notes that younger generations are moving more toward less formal spiritualties, not just in the Black Church but globally. They cross denominations and often renounce institutionalized religion. African-Americans are not monolithic in theologies; however, due to common African roots, unity in diversity exists. There is a spiritual connection among African-Americans that transcends denominations and even faiths. A unique spirituality in African-American women is to create their own welfare systems to help others.

Hayes points out that the relevance is the substance of African-American spirituality in the African-American experience, always alongside social justice. The forging in the fiery furnace continued through the Jim Crow era, the civil rights movement, Black nationalism, and the present-day grassroots movement. In current times, people of Christian roots are drifting away from Christianity into self-proclaimed spiritualties. If this be the case, especially for African-Americans, the spirituality will no longer evolve; African-Americans will no longer be forged in the fiery furnace that grows their faith (2002).

Concepts from Howard Thurman

Thurman focuses on prayer and mystical experiences in the African-American traditions. His discussion reveals a strong connection of artistic ability in African-American spirituality. For example, the articulation of the black preacher's words gave slaves the endurance to live through struggles. Also, lyrics of spirituals referenced the Old and New Testaments, the world of nature, and the common personal experiences of the slave, focusing on deliverance of the wrongfully oppressed. The significance to the dissertation thesis is that the preacher, like the gospel artist, is uniquely empowered by his or her artistic ability in articulation to deliver the Christian message of hope and transformation. It may be a "hoop" style or mere poetic delivery that captivates the crowd (1975).

Thurman analyzes the lyrical content of various spirituals and notes that one attitude found in Negro spirituals is that some things in life are worse than death. In general, life is viewed as an experience of evil, frustration, and despair. One mood focuses on the loneliness and discouragement of life. He points out that the theme of personal commitment to life and sojourning the pilgrimage have been common in black sacred music (1975).

The significance of this point to this dissertation thesis is that as the theoretical chords and technical aspects of black sacred music evolve, the theme of encouragement and endurance transcends all styles. Black sacred music must leave the listener and the deliverer inspired through trials, tribulations, and triumphs. The gospel artist ministering today must continue to be effective with this ability to touch souls.

Concepts of James Cone

The primary theme of Cone's text is that the spirituals and the blues are about the power of song in the struggle for black survival. Cone interprets spirituals from the perspective of liberation theology. Throughout the text, he connects the lyrics of spirituals to black eschatology. The spirituals convey that God has not left the slaves alone and that God will deliver them from human bondage (1991).

Cone analyzes the blues and calls them secular spirituals, based on the themes of both trouble and suffering. Music is the core of daily life in Africa, a trait noted in the development of spirituals and blues. It later became evident in various genres of black music. The music of African-American people all sums up to be "soul" music. It is all sung from the souls of black folk. A measure of effectiveness for gospel music and by-product genres is that it must reach from soul to soul (1991).

This research provides an opportunity to synthesize African-American spirituality from inception to current times from a Christian perspective. Reference Table 17, included in the Appendix 2, is a user-friendly tool for assessing the content and outcomes discussed concerning African-American spiritualty.

Additionally, Robert E. Webber discusses African-American theology of worship. He states that it came out of a deep sense of oppression and a high anticipation for liberation. Furthermore, when in worship, African-Americans experience the liberating redeeming power of Jesus Christ, delivering them from sin and the power of the evil one. Despite the denomination, the African-American Christian community has a common understanding of God's initiative in the call to worship. Worshipers come just as they are to give thanks and seek forgiveness, wholeness, liberation, and empowerment in a society of oppression. He explains that the uniqueness of the African-American theology is the "liberation key" established in the brush harbors filled with African-American spirituals. The brush harbors evolved to edifices filled with varied forms of gospel music and metered hymns. The liberating key is evident in the African primal world view and led early folk theologians to seek separate places of worship.

The Preaching of the Black Church (Dr. Luke Powery)

The sermon of the African-American church tradition was preluded by the songs of the congregation and choir. The Homiletics, Hymns and Spirituals Conference held in Charlotte in 2011 reviewed the role of celebration and lamentation in African-American preaching. In this seminar, Dr. Luke Powery explained the theology of lamentation and celebration in the African-American worship experience.

Dr. Powery began this session by first explaining that homiletics is the art of preaching about a scriptural teaching. In the African-American culture, the preacher delivers sermonic points and reaches a celebrative style that includes musical pitches, vocal inflections, a rhythmic pattern, elongated vowels, dynamic changes, and even poetic license of the language. This is accompanied by back-up music—primarily on an organ, but a full church band can partake in the delivery. Some refer to this preaching style as "whooping" the sermon. This occurs at the end of the sermon to touch the hearts of the congregation, just as gospel singers seek to touch the hearts of listeners. This style of delivery can be practiced during preparation; however, whooping includes spontaneous call-and-response interaction and improvisation. Dr. Powery pointed out that there are two style of worship: lamentation and celebration. The celebrative style cannot be appreciated without understanding lamentation. This is the foundation of praise, the tear before a smile, or the groan in our gospel. Attendees gathered that the lament that occurs before a celebration is significant in giving more substance to a cause for celebration. It is the trial before a triumph and therefore deserves an in-depth analysis (Dr. Luke Powery, personal communication, Feb. 17, 2012).

Lamentation

In Dr. Powery's lecture, he asked, "Does your gospel groan?" He began the lecture by singing a centering song to set the tone for his lecture before he explained the importance of lamentation. The *Merriam Webster Dictionary* defines a *lamentation* as an expression of great sorrow or deep sadness. One may ask, what is the significance of having "groan" in gospel? (Dr. Luke Powery, personal communication, Feb. 17, 2012).

He began the lamentation explanation by first pointing out that there is a rich historical connection between preaching and music in the African-American church. He asked, "Do we know what came first, the spirituals or the sermons?" In *God's Trombone,* James Weldon discusses preaching and music. *God's Trombone* is a book of poems of seven Negro sermons written in the tradition of African-American religious oratory. In a more contemporary view, Dr. Powery stated that gospel artist and pastor Shirley Caesar says she sings her sermons and preaches her songs. These examples set the stage for his evaluation of what he called the "two sides of the homiletical coin" (Dr. Luke Powery, personal communication, Feb. 17, 2012).

Lamentation is the lows and celebration is the highs. Before one goes up and celebrates, he or she must go to the lows. This is the paradox of the gospel and Christian worship. As Christians, we cannot celebrate until we know how to lament. For us to become doxologians, where our primary purpose is to worship God in the good and the bad times, we must understand the biblical and theological roots of lamentation (Dr. Luke Powery, personal communication, Feb. 17, 2012).

Before he explained the biblical text on lamentation, Dr. Powery discussed further the importance of understanding groaning praise. He pointed out that doxology means two things: *doca* ("glory") and *logy* ("word or expression"). He pointed out how ecstasy (in groan) and glory exist together. Next, he reminded the attendees that in contemporary music, one must be careful of the notion conveyed by the praise and worship genre. This musical genre is commercialized and conveys the concept that when "praises go up, blessings come down," a phrase often chanted in the African-American church. Dr. Powery called this "candy theology" because this not a realistic expectation. The realistic expectation is that life has groans and sadness. It is not always a celebration. Praise must still go up even when blessings do not come down. Christians will experience trials and tribulations even when praises are going up to God. Third, the foundation of our praise is pain, suffering, and agony. We often mask reality with church chants and common phrases like "I am blessed and highly favored." How do we praise without becoming disconnected from our reality? Does your gospel groan? (Dr. Luke Powery, personal communication, Feb. 17, 2012).

The biblical references for this discussion on lamentation began with a look at Romans 8: 18–39. Verses 18–30 (NIV) cover present suffering and future glory and explain how they do not compare with the glory of God.

Dr. Powery described lamenting as faithful speech, Christian worship out of a groaning. Psalms have been called the songs of the spirit and convey that trouble does not last always. Jesus lamented when He suffered on the cross at His crucifixion. The cross reveals that the Spirit is present even in death and human suffering. The wounds remain and are not erased, even after the resurrection. The marks of suffering are present. Lamentation acknowledges this. Dr. Powery mentioned that the book *African-American Christian Worship* states that the denial of lament in the Christian life is a denial of African-American history, of the Holy Spirit, and of the Christian life and reality (Dr. Luke Powery, personal communication, Feb. 17, 2012).

As a demonstration of the connection between African-American homiletics and music, in the lamentation aspect, Dr. Powery broke out singing "Soon a Will Be Done" from his soul. This is one of many Negro spirituals written with lyrics that illustrate the "groan" in slaves' praise of God.

He reminded the audience, who had all lived the African-American church experience, that a key ingredient in the Black Church worship style comes from the cultural and social experience of African-American history. The lamenting times in our personal history are released to God in our gospel. This is what creates the "testimony" for those who sing gospel music. The laments in life are the tests we must pass. Passing these tests and tribulations allows us to attest to how being steadfast and faithful in our Christianity has allowed us to overcome our past. In the African-American church, the laments are creatively and soulfully delivered by song or sermon, reaching the hearts of the listeners (Dr. Luke Powery, personal communication, Feb. 17, 2012).

Celebration

Dr. Powery transitioned from praise of lamentation to praise in celebration by first noting Romans chapter 8. It speaks to the sufferings of the present time and how they cannot be compared with the glory about to be revealed. Paul ends chapter 8 with a full-blown doxology (groaning praise). Similarly, Dr. Powery points out how "Nobody Knows the Trouble I've Seen" has a refrain ending in "Glory, hallelujah." He stated, "Even in celebration, we don't let go of the groan." Celebration is deeply rooted in the resurrection of Jesus Christ, the "ascent," the going up. Going down, before going up, has a bittersweet tension (Dr. Luke Powery, personal communication, Feb. 17, 2012).

He referenced the book called *Preaching with Sacred Fire,* by Martha Simmons. This book takes a historical look at whooping, the artistic delivery of sermons known to the African-American church. It includes an African-American preacher named Charles Adams, trained at Harvard and known as the "Harvard whooper." Adams described shouting as a rendezvous with God, a rendezvous with love, yielding an out-of-body experience.

Henry Mitchell in *Celebration & Experience in Preaching* discusses how authentic gospel feasting is a celebration. One cannot be high on Jesus and do nothing for humanity. Celebration in preaching should inspire us to go out and share the good news with humanity. Celebration alone does not present a true preaching, and lamentation alone is not healthy. We need doxology, which is celebration and lamentation (Dr. Luke Powery, personal communication, Feb. 17, 2012).

The Connection between Preaching and Music in the African-American Tradition

In addition to the connection between preaching and music that occurs during the sermonic delivery is the overall connection for the complete service. The music ministry must complement the efforts of the pastor and others leading the service. The conference discussed seven characteristics of preaching and music. These are outlined and compiled as they were conveyed by Dr. Powery.

1) The cross of Christ is the focus. This has to do with the postures of worship. Worshipers must remember why they are doing this in the first place. The ultimate aim is to be doxologians.

2) Congruency is important. The music must be on the same page with the pastor. The preaching and music must have a marriage. The music must not be disconnected and be in a silo. It should be an undertone accompanying the sermon. Worship is not just the music; it is the complete connection and offering to God.

3) Communication must occur prior to the service and during the service. The pastor is the worship leader.

4) Collaboration must occur between the pastor and music ministry. The planning is a collaborative effort.

5) Compromise must occur sometimes in order to move forward.

6) Care is important. Pastor and musician leadership must care for each other, as a child of God.

7) Congregational ministry is important. Powery stated, "We must reclaim the service of worship as a ministry. It must minister to those in the pews. We must be sure the context of the music speaks to the climate of the church."

CHAPTER 3

Literature Review of the Historical Development of Gospel Music

The Approach to the Literature Review

As the socioeconomic circumstances of African-Americans evolved, so did the needs and desires sought from the Black Church worship experience. "Having church" evolved to worship space and a worship experience beyond the four walls of the church. This study focuses on gospel music; however, secular genres of blues/jazz music and other cultural artistic expressions also evolved with the plight of the African-American.

A thematic and chronological review of African-American church music explains the evolution of gospel music as well as the worship space. The chronological review provides historical developments in black sacred music, which evolved to stylistic variations of gospel music from 1930 to 2015. Understanding the precursory events in African-American history that planted the seed for its evolution needs to take place before focusing on the development of gospel music. This approach provides the basis for understanding how the platform for ministry grew from secret worship in plantation hush arbors, often referred to as the invisible institution, to commercialized venues in concert arenas, auditoriums, and airwaves. This commercialized venue is the gospel music industry that evolved alongside the development of gospel music. The chronological trace of black sacred music primarily leverages relevant research and contributions by scholars Raymond Wise, Eileen Southern, C. Eric Lincoln, and Lawrence Mamiya, along with compiled works by Dr. James Abbington and interviews and webinars with Professor L. Stanley Davis. The angle from which each of them researched and presented their work provides the understanding essential for gaining foundational knowledge of black sacred music. Therefore, this study is not intended to be an exhaustive historical perspective of African-American church music and worship. The emphasis of this section is on the pertinent contributions that are milestones toward the evolution of the gospel genre and art form in the music industry. This literature review enables an effective synthesis of ideas and theories for future contributions. How did cultural expressions birthed out of the pain and misery of slavery evolve to an art form that has mass appeal in cross-cultural worship space and the marketplace of the music and entertainment industry? The following sections answer this question. Each section reviews a chronological segment of the black sacred music timeline, a brief commentary on the African-American historical parallel, and a synoptic overview of the black sacred music contributions at that stage.

A summary of each section is included in the assessment of the scholarly literature discussed in chapter 5, "Presentation and Analysis." Tables detail a summary of the milestones on the path of the emerging gospel genre, art form, practices, venues, and controversies that were overcome to develop the gospel music industry.

Pre-Gospel Era (Pre-1900), Pre- and Post-Emancipation Ditties, Hollers, and Spirituals

Some scholars such as Eric Lincoln and Lawrence H. Mamiya do not include the pre-1900 time frame in the pre-gospel era. They refer to it as the spiritual era and start pre-gospel at 1900. For the sake of this research, all activities and contributions prior to the development years of gospel music are included in this section.

The historical parallel for this section covers the 1700s to late 1865 (pre-emancipation), 1865–1877, the reconstruction of the US following the Civil War, and the 1865 emancipation of slavery. Throughout the history of African-Americans, the socioeconomic conditions impacted the cultural expressions of each period. The first evidence of this is found during the slavery era, 1619–1865. A visual of this timeline is housed in the gospel music history archives of the University of Southern California (USC) Libraries online (2015).

Enslaved Africans brought with them to this strange land their own authentic expressions of song and dance. The oppressive state of slavery yielded the earliest form of African-American worship music, often referred to as "ditties," in the late 1700s. These songs were close in form to the song and dance of the African origins of the enslaved and preceded what would eventually form the world-renowned genre of Negro spirituals. The original spirituals sung by slaves while working the fields are referred to as folk spirituals, distinguishing them from the concert style spirituals known as Negro spirituals. They were the earlier form of indigenous a cappella religious music created by African-Americans during slavery (Burnim and Maultsby, 2006). Slaves on southern plantations often sang these moans and groans in secrecy. During this time, most slaves were not considered practicing Christians, and the ditties were associated with their native religious practices. At this point, few slave owners were introducing Christianity to their slaves for fear that becoming Christians would make them feel they were equal to whites. Worship songs and work songs were often interchangeable as both were expressions to boost morale, and slave owners used them to help keep track of slaves. Field hollers, as work songs were often called, were not separated out in slave culture because the African worldview was holistic and had no concept of secular singing (Burnim and Maultsby, 2006). Singing was viewed as a way of harmonizing with nature, and no distinction was made between the spiritual and secular expressions, according to gospel music enthusiast/online journalist Michael Tanner (2015) in his article "Crosscurrents: A Brief history of Gospel Music." According to PBS's *The Slave Experience: Education, Arts, & Culture,* slaves manufactured and played a variety of instruments. Singing and dancing occurred during the little leisure time they had to participate in secular and sacred activities. Some slaveholders were amused by the talent of the African-Americans. Others forbade the singing and dancing because they feared the activity would incite a rebellion. For this reason, in South Carolina in 1739, the playing of drums was prohibited for fear that the rhythms would be used to communicate subversive activity (PBS, 2004).

The Second Great Awakening, 1790s–1830s, was a period of large-scale revival and camp meetings led by Baptist and Methodist preachers throughout the nation. Slave owners and slaves alike were encouraged to convert to Christianity and eradicate sin in the name of perfectionism. Eileen Southern's research revealed that the Negro spirituals came out of the camp meeting phenomenon, often consisting of thousands of slaves during the Second Awakening. Slaves were preached to by their slave owners, attended service with their slave owners, or had worship services supervised by whites. Although some slave owners were reluctant to offer Christianity to slaves, others saw it as a way to maintain submission (Southern, 1997).

Hearing biblical text influenced the birth of what is known as the Negro spiritual. The text of many spirituals had biblical references about deliverance from oppression. Dr. Raymond Wise points out that the spirituals fell primarily into three categories: slow (for sad events), metered, and jubilee (upbeat) for happiness and fast shouts. The fast shouts often accompanied the ring shout that slaves conducted in the praise house where they were allowed to worship. Negro spirituals are referred to by the Library of Congress as one of the largest and most significant forms of American folk songs. Their lyrics express remnants of slave daily life, and biblical references to freedom in heaven were common themes. Spirituals expressed the souls, thoughts, few joys, and many pains of slave life. Some also were used for escape codes for activities such as those led by Harriett Tubman in the Underground Railroad (Negro Spirituals, 2015).

As slaves and freed African-Americans began to develop their own churches, spirituals were sung by the congregation, often led by the singing preacher or other naturally gifted psalmists of the church. This occurred before the end of slavery. According to scholar Dr. Wendell Whalum of Morehouse College, spirituals became the musical basis for all later church music. The Negro spiritual laid the basic foundation for subsequent forms of black sacred and secular music alike. As the number of black ministers grew, so did the distinctions of styles of worship in the Black Church. Two main paths began to develop in the form of black worship: the spontaneous and emotional versus the conservative and structured. This led to a dichotomy that would guide the development of black sacred music in the years to come (Wise, 2002).

In 1871, the Fisk Jubilee Singers began touring and singing to white audiences a new sophisticated version of Negro spirituals that had been westernized by applying European choral part voicing (Wise, 2002). These were anthem concertized spirituals that were noticeably different in sound from slave spirituals sung in the fields to sooth the oppressive conditions of slave life (personal communication, Davis, Nov. 10, 2015). Their touring was initially local in Nashville, where the school resided. The concept was an idea of George L. White, a young white professor who was the school's treasurer and music instructor. They eventually travelled internationally, singing Negro spirituals (Fisk Jubilee Singers, 2015).

Congregational singing was the dominant format of worship for the early African-American worshipers in the early established black churches. This was adapted from the exposure to European style worship and the use of hymns. Bethel A.M.E Church in Philadelphia was one of the first black churches to have a choir. This occurred between 1841 and 1842, as hymn singing was promoted by Bishop Daniel Payne between the years of 1811 and 1893. He denounced the slave-style spirituals, field hollers, ring shouts, and other expressions of African heritage in worship. Payne sought every opportunity to prove the capability of the African to function in America and saw these activities as ignorant, based on the standards and expectations set by white Methodist clergy (Wise, 2002).

The hymns of Isaac Watts were popularized by black Methodists and Baptists alike, and they were sung in a rendition more akin to African-American culture with call and response and in rhythm. During this era, printed hymnals were limited, and not everyone could read. The tradition called "lining" the hymn was usually led by one of the deacons. The deacon would lead first by speaking one line of the hymn in metered format. Next, it was sung by the congregation, a cappella and in harmony. Blacks adapted the tradition they learned from their European slave owner's worship style with their own "flavor" to the musical style (Lincoln and Mamiya, 1990). Shaped note singing became a style adapted from the European Sacred Harp singing of the *fa so ti do* scale called four-shaped note singing. Black church congregations adopted a version of this for the Black Church community, and their shaped note singing included spirituals. A seven-shaped-note style eventually evolved that is believed to have developed from the black gospel tradition (Wise, 2002). A summary of this section is included in the assessment of the scholarly literature discussed in this era. Refer to chapter 5, "Presentation and Analysis," for further details about how this era planted the seed and contributed to the gospel music industry.

Pre-Gospel Era (1900–1920), Empowerment by Education Negro Spirituals/Anthems

The early twentieth century, 1900–1930, is used by scholars Mellonee Burnim and Portia Maultsby as the scope of what occurred next toward the evolution of gospel music. It is referred to as the transitional era, based on the start of Charles A. Tindley's pioneering gospel style. This rural gospel style was a sacred counterpart of the blues and was influenced by the Holiness-Pentecostal worship of the Church of God in Christ. This era overlaps with what is discussed in this section up to 1920.

After the emancipation of slavery in 1865, blacks would begin a journey in search of equality and full benefits of American citizenship that would last decades, with steady strides being made yet with occasional violations. Reconstruction was an attempt by the federal government to jumpstart this journey for African-Americans. Nonetheless, resistance to change by white supremacy thoughts created separation and inequality. African-Americans sought education as empowerment and as the key to opportunity to overcome these socioeconomic challenges. This new mind-set was demonstrated in the transitional phase of African-American worship and sacred music (Reagon, 1992).

Westernized spirituals grew in popularity as classics and were sung by more historically black colleges such as Morehouse and Tuskegee Institute. The Fisk Jubilee Singers even reached notoriety by recording "There is a Balm in Gilead" in 1909, as stated in Jerma A. Jackson's *Singing in My Soul*. Funding for historically black colleges was needed to provide education opportunities for blacks. Jubilee singing became a popular means for raising funds and was received as a well-respected art form among blacks and whites. As blacks became more educated and skilled, new pioneering composers documented their interpretations of the spirituals. Their actions allowed Negro spirituals to influence other genres and to gain their position as a classic American treasure (Reagon, 1992).

Harry T. Burleigh was recognized for publishing arrangements for spirituals for a solo voice. He graduated from the National Conservatory of Music in 1896 and was well known for singing spirituals while he worked, cleaning the conservatory halls. This practice would eventually afford him international fame as it drew the attention of the conservatory's director, Czech composer Antonín Dvořák. They established a working association, and the spirituals that Burleigh shared with Dvořák influenced his *Symphony from the New World* and the beginning of each movement of the *American String Quartet*. Dvořák applied the pentatonic scale he learned from studying spirituals with Burleigh; this scale was common to spirituals and Native American music. Burleigh broke race barriers when he was employed by or permitted to share his baritone voice at churches and synagogues that traditionally did not allow blacks to worship with them. In 1914, Burleigh was a founding member of the American Society of Composers, Authors and Publishers (ASCAP), where he would eventually sit on the board in 1941. In 1916 and 1917, Burleigh published several versions of "Deep River" and continued to be well known for his spirituals and art songs for voice and piano (Southern, 1997).

An increasing number of whites began to show an interest in the classical style of Negro spirituals. The appreciation of spirituals and what were often called jubilee songs was quickly recognized for profitability by white publishing companies that sold these songs on sheet music. Eileen Southern points out that a surge in sheet music sales occurred during this era, which helped expose Negro spiritual arrangements to white audiences (Southern, 1997).

Anthems were introduced to the Black Church by Nathaniel Dett in 1914 and 1916. Nathaniel Dett's claim to fame was his ability to set folk songs and spirituals to choral and piano compositions in the romantic style. He was a classically trained pianist and considered one of the most successful black composers of his era. Dett graduated from Lane College in 1907 with a Bachelor of Music Degree and continued his education at Oberlin Conservatory of Music and Harvard University. He would eventually perform at Carnegie Hall and the Boston Symphony Hall as a guest pianist and choral director. He was among the earliest black composers to have a membership in ASCAP. His contributions also include teaching for 20 years at Hampton Institute, establishing the Hampton Institute Choral Union and the Hampton School of Music. He would go on to publish *Religious Folksongs of the Negro* (1927) and *The Dett Collections of Negro Spirituals* (1936).

Development (1920s–1930s) and Traditional Gospel Era (1930–1945) The Harlem Renaissance /New Negro Movement Gospel Hymnody/Gospel Genre

Some scholars trace 1900–1930 or 1910–1930, aligned with the first great migration of blacks to the North, as a transitional period. They then overlap 1930–1945 (traditional gospel era) into the early part of the next era, the golden age, from 1945 to 1967 (Davis, 2015). Wise and Southern segment the 1920s–1930s as the era of development for the gospel music genre and the movement away from spirituals as the premier black sacred music, circa the time of the Harlem Renaissance. Regardless of how it is scoped, the outcome from 1910–1945 was that the music derived from spirituals and hymns set to blues progressions had become a sustainable traditionalized genre called gospel music.

The Harlem Renaissance took place in the Harlem district of New York City approximately 1919–1933. This decade in African-American history was a flourishing of cultural expressions in the form of visual art, photography, theater, music, and literary and scholastic intellect that fostered a new black identity. This period in American history was originally called the New Negro Movement, based on the work of anthropologist Alain Locke. There existed a renewed "race-spirit" that resulted from resistance to self-denial, impatience for equality, and perseverance through political suppression and socioeconomic disparities of the Negro American. The plight of the emancipated Negro obtained a sudden interest by whites in America. This era was in the midst of the First Great Migration (1910–1930), when 1.6 million blacks from the South migrated north and west in search of job opportunities and better living conditions in industrial cities. Blacks sought to "re-brand" what it meant to be black in America (Rowan and Brunner, 2015). The Garvey Movement, pan-Africanism, and Black nationalism all contributed to the new mind-set to embrace African heritage and to resist assimilation. The impact was noted in the more conscious black American (Salzman, 1993). Work songs and field hollers birthed blues, which evolved before 1900 out of the frustrations of common black life. Blues birthed ragtime and now a new folk music called jazz. It was bright, vibrant, upbeat, and hopeful. In the same manner, 17th-century cornfield ditties begot 18th-century spirituals that spoke of the oppressive state of slavery and a longing for heaven. Spirituals evolved from improvisation to structured harmonies, eventually intertwined with anthems and hymnody. The new arrival had been birthed and was called gospel music. It had an encouraging lyric that spoke to enduring the struggle on earth (Southern, 1997).

A new era was launched in Black Church music in the 1930s with a style of singing that came from the folk, the newly settled Negros. It was often created spontaneously and was similar to the style of the folk spiritual. This was common to the congregations that evolved out of the Azuza Street Revivals, from 1906 to 1908, using instrumentation such as horns, mandolins, and jugs, which were not accepted by the Baptists and Methodists (Burnim and Maultsby, 2006). This style was evident in the Church of God in Christ and Pentecostal and Holiness churches, following the social migration of blacks from the South to the North. The preacher, song leader, and congregation were all often involved in on-the-spot song creation (Wise, 2002). Davis notes that the Church of God in Christ demonstrated early traits of gospel music in its congregational singing. However, it was not yet "coined" as gospel. It consisted of the call-and-response format; it was highly participatory, simple, and repetitive (personal communication Davis, 2015).

Rev. Charles A. Tindley gained popularity in the Black Church community as a preacher- singer in the Methodist tradition for his contributions to gospel hymnody. This was the new song genre that spoke to the needs of the common people of the African-American community in the rapidly growing urban cities of the North. He wrote, performed, and published songs that depicted the oppression of African-Americans who migrated north. Their theme brought encouragement to those surviving the worldly circumstances of the time (Wise, 2002).

Tindley and his church, Tindley Temple United Methodist Church of Philadelphia, became well known for concerts and new music. Burnim and Maultsby (2006) explain that Tindley had been influenced by the post-Civil War doctrines of the Holiness Movement, which had resulted from an interdenominational effort led by Methodists whose aim was to reinvigorate their worship. Tindley Temple often had congregational singing with extemporaneous prayers akin to the worship practices of slaves. The songs he wrote complemented his sermons in a call-and-response structure with space in the melodic line, as Horace Boyer noted, for improvisation of text, melody or the blues third and seventh notes, best learned by performance practice instead of notation.

He was paving the way for the "singer-preacher" concept as a traveling artist of the Black Church, and he created a venue where appreciation for worship music outside of morning services could be fostered. This was done by using gospel hymns for informal services, not morning worship, where Protestant hymns and anthems were used. He passed away in 1933 and did not live to see the sustainability of the gospel genre (Wise, 2002).

White gospel hymnody was a product of the Protestant City Revival Movement (Southern, 1997), from the late 19th century, which focused on a style similar in harmony to barbershop singing. The white composers generally used major keys, I, IV, V progressions, straightforward rhythms, and harmonies. These songs were easier to sing than the traditional hymn styles, and white composers' hymns would gain popularity with blacks, who attended segregated camp revivals. In the early 1900s Homer Rodeheaver was a traveling lead singer for Billy Sunday, who published gospel collections with great favorites like "The Old Rugged Cross," by George Bernard (Wise, 2002).

Dr. Wise (2002) explains how the *Gospel Pearls* hymnal played a major role in the spreading and acceptance of gospel music into the black denominational churches throughout the nation. Published in 1921, this was the first hymnal released specifically for black churches. It included gospel music favorites of white composers and black composers alike. Some of the white composers included were Ira Sankey (known for "Yield Not to Temptation"), William Doane, and Charles Gabriel (known for "His Eye is On the Sparrow"). Some of the African-American composers were Charles Tindley, Lucie Campbell, and Thomas Dorsey. *Gospel Pearls* would eventually provide common grounds of cross-denominational hymnody to the Baptist, Methodist, and Pentecostal worship styles.

Lucie Campbell, known for "Touch Me, Lord Jesus" and "Footprints of Jesus," was primarily a self-taught musician who grew to impressive proficiency. She was educated in liberal arts at Rust College in her home state, Mississippi. She played a pivotal role in providing a platform for exposure of the early gospel composer through her influence and position in the National Baptist Convention. She was the first major African-American female composer of gospel hymns. In 1916, she was appointed as music director of the National Baptist Convention and provided the avenue of exposure of gospel hymns to the African-American Church community (Wise, 2002).

Campbell provided the opportunity for Thomas Dorsey to gain great exposure via the National Baptist Convention, where he heard the great works of Charles Tindley and decided to focus his writing abilities full time on gospel songs. Dorsey grew up in church yet had achieved a successful career as a blues and jazz pianist by the name of "Georgia Tom" (Wise, 2002).

In approximately 1930 in Chicago, Dorsey began merging blues and protest hymns with simple spiritual lyrics in an innovative arrangement. This style was a fusion between sacred and secular music. Professor L. Stanley Davis, an internationally recognized scholar in academia of black sacred music, defines gospel music as the following equation: gospel music = blues + Anglo-Saxton Protestant hymns.

The National Convention of Gospel Choirs and Choruses (NCGCC) was established in 1933 from a gospel choir union at Pilgrim Baptist Church in Chicago, under the leadership of Thomas A. Dorsey. He was the first to refer to this new "soul music" as gospel songs. This gospel union evolved to a conference for the collective betterment of the Christian singer, instrumentalists, educators, and leaders. It would eventually become a platform for talented gospel composers, musicians, and artists to gain exposure and spread their music to black churches. Raymond Wise explains that Dorsey became known as "the father of gospel music" because of his musicianship, which combined the musical elements of secular and sacred styles that formed a hybrid product. It was important to Dorsey to use the term *gospel songs* to distinguish the different styles of sacred music of the Black Church and to distinguish the gospel hymns from the Protestant revival movement of the 19th century (Wise, 2002).

Evolution from the cylinder record to the vinyl record in the late 1920s and radio were media that helped spread various musical genres, including blues and gospel. According to Raymond Wise, radio, which had become a major source of entertainment in the 1920s, focused on the white middle class. Sunday morning broadcasts included sanctified-style worship from small storefront congregations. Preachers, congregations, and quartet groups on radio broadcasts reached blacks and whites. Eventually white record companies were drawn to marketing black music to whites for the "race" record audience (Wise, 2002).

The topic of quartet singing in black sacred music deserves an extensive study of its own to capture an extensive look at the implications and contributions from numerous groups. Many thrived well with local and regional notoriety that earned them income. Horace Clarence Boyer (1995) sparks the interest for further research in *The Golden Age of Gospel*. He explains that while Pentecostal/Holiness churches developed the unique style of worship and singing and the series of blind and sighted church singers who travelled with preachers, the quartet groups emerged from the workplace. They sang the jubilee style of singing that many learned from college at historically black colleges and universities (HBCUs). When they graduated from college they returned to the community and taught others at work or in the community to sing Negro spirituals and gospel hymns a cappella in jubilee style. The Fisk Jubilee Quartet, a by-product of the Fisk Jubilee Singers, is an example. The popularity of quartet groups quickly spread among black men and became a favorite past time. They operated like a structured club with officers, rules, dues, and regular rehearsals. They wore uniforms and planned formal singing engagements. The early Baptist jubilee quartet singing was conservative and poised, like popular barbershop singing. They did not want the reputation of the "holy roller" Pentecostal singers, yet the crowd response began to set the atmosphere for the Pentecostal style influence (Boyer, 1995).

Various types of quartet singing began to evolve regionally, and families and communities became known to have well-established quartet singing dynasties. One mentioned by Boyer is The Foster Singers from Bessemer, Alabama, the first black quartet to transition the sound from European-influenced university style singing to the more current day "folk" style gospel quartet. Their impact on quartet singing in Alabama was significant. Other groups spread across the South, including the Silver Leaf Quartets, Harmonizing Four, the Golden Gate Quartet of the Virginia tidewater area, and the Dixie Hummingbirds of Greenville, South Carolina (Boyer, 1995).

Quartet groups were emerging with a style of jubilee singing to a gospel style with instrumental accompaniment, instead of a cappella, that included using a "swing lead" technique. A different soloist sang a stanza instead of the same leader for the entire song. Other key practices included adding the fifth singer to a quartet and ad-libbing with repetitive sounds, a style started by the Soul Stirrers. Sam Cooke is accredited with introducing this. Falsetto singing was first introduced by Claude Jeter of the Swan Silvertones. The quartet group fused the freestyle collective improvisation of the Black Church and the rhetorical solo style of the gospel preacher. These practices of quartet singing influenced the performance practices of other gospel music as well.

Quartet groups contributed to the emerging gospel music industry. They established a following that supported them with paid performances. Local groups became regional and national professional gospel artists, eventually allowing some to tour and sing as fulltime professionals (Wise, 2002).

Evidence of the emerging gospel music industry began to take shape as Dorsey's business acumen in music, which he gained from blues and jazz, revolutionized gospel music. Chicago became the "birthplace of gospel music" because Dorsey and his gospel pioneers/colleagues moved there or frequented the city. It was a hub for gospel music expression, and churches in Chicago permitted gospel choirs to organize. Others feared gospel choirs would eliminate congregational singing. Chicago was to gospel music what Detroit has been to the automotive industry and what Los Angeles has been to the television and film industry. The key influences and songwriters of gospel music resided in Chicago, and it was at the National Baptist Convention in 1930 that the promotion of gospel music occurred. The convention became the vehicle for disseminating new material across music ministries at black churches. For example, at this same session of the convention, when Dorsey's composition "If You See My Savior" was performed live, he sold 4,000 copies (Wise, 2002).

Dorsey, along with Lucie Campbell, eventually gained exposure of their music by publishing it and selling sheet music. Scored music was the primary distribution method of gospel music. He established Dorsey House of Music in 1932, which was the first music publishing company dedicated to selling gospel music by black gospel composers. Dorsey himself wrote approximately 1,000 songs and published 500 of them. He is best known for "Precious Lord, Take My Hand," "Peace in the Valley," and "Search Me, Lord." He also continued to be an active blues pianist and writer while being a successful gospel composer. He used the flatted thirds, seventh, and bent tones (Wise, 2002).

Dorsey travelled the country providing live demonstrations of the music he wrote and published for sale on sheet music. It was difficult to capture the feel and intricacies of gospel music on paper. For demonstration, Dorsey trained and worked with Sallie Martin, Willie Mae Ford Smith, and the infamous Mahalia Jackson as primary soloist. Each of these soloists offered impactful contributions in their style and creativity to the music and in sponsorship and training of others. Sallie Martin and Dorsey organized more than 500 Baptist gospel groups. Gospel music comes from the oral tradition of African roots, and eventually playing it by ear and learning by rote became easier than learning complex sheet music. They helped transfer the style for delivering the song via hands-on teaching and live demonstration. This was primarily through the National Baptist Convention and Dorsey's National Convention of Gospel Choirs and Choruses. Dorsey created the template for artist development by having his accomplished singers develop and train others. Willie Mae Ford Smith, who was known for bringing vocal runs to gospel, met a beautician named Mahalia Jackson. They met during her Soloist Bureau held during a Dorsey Convention. She taught her techniques to 100 soloists. Mahalia found an instant connection and eventually decided to leave the beauty shop to pursue singing professionally. These practices of live demonstration and teaching gospel to choirs, soloists, and groups at Dorsey's convention also paved the road for formatting gospel music promotion in a system that Dorsey established. The system would become a practice that foretold of the gospel music industry (Wise, 2002).

During the 1920s and 1930s, Southern's research identified two distinct groups other than soloists that had emerged in gospel music: all-male quartet groups of four or five men dressed to impress in full suits, and all female choirs, who wore choir robes. The quartets sang a capella barbershop-style harmony, with percussions from finger snapping to thigh slapping. The choruses sang to piano accompaniment with hands clapping while some had tambourines. Singing evangelists, soloists, and groups toured the church circuit for various types of worship services, both formal and informal. These services included special occasions, concerts, regular weekly services, and Sunday afternoon programs that were more like entertainment. It was generally acceptable to lift a no-obligation offering for these programs (Southern, 1997).

Dorsey changed the mind-set of "free gospel music" when he promoted a "battle of song" in 1936 with Roberta and Sallie Martin. The host site was Chicago DuSable High School. The entry charge was 15 cents. This is documented as the first time there was a charge at a black sacred music concert, other than that of the Fisk Jubilee Singers. This practice set the pace and professionalism for gospel music. Charging admission helped propel gospel music to greater stages and venues alongside secular music. The singers were able to get paid for their talent. A follow-up event, which moved gospel music to new venues, was Rosetta Thorpe's performance at the world-famous Cotton Club on the Cab Calloway show. She sang and played her guitar and became the first gospel singer to sign to a major commercial company (Decca Records). Gospel music was no longer just for church people (Southern, 1997). In 1938, Rosetta Thorpe's hit "This Train" became the first gospel record to sell one million copies (USC Digital Library, 2015).

Golden Age of Gospel (1945–Mid-1960s) 1960–1967 Modern Traditional Included) Post-World War II

It was during the golden age of gospel that early signs of the gospel artist were more evident and began to emerge. Some scholars include an overlap here called the modern traditional era, from 1960 to 1967. This is explained in *The Black Church in the African-American Experience,* by C. Eric Lincoln and Lawrence H. Mamiya (1990). Prior to this era, worship services consisted primarily of congregation hymns, to which Tindley contributed greatly. Dorsey, Lucie Campbell, Sallie Martin, Roberta Martin, and others were instrumental in transforming the congregational gospel hymns by Tindley into arrangements for church choirs, soloists, and ensembles. Some of the famous vocalists who sang these arrangements included Mahalia Jackson, the Dixie Hummingbirds, the Five Blind Boys of Mississippi, and the Sensational Nightingales. The congregation moved from participants to observers as an audience. The congregation became more bystanders, whose participation was now affirming verbally with responses or physically by movement, clapping, or limited singing. Lincoln and Mamiya refer to this change in roles and experience as a sociological consequence. They noted that black worshipers and concert-goers became the audiences to a new homiletical gospel experience (Lincoln and Mamiya, 1990).

A venue that served as a gospel circuit for specialized ensembles and talented soloists emerged. Gospel music continued to be criticized by some black churches as blues disguised in spiritual dress. Sociologist E. Franklin Frazier noted that some more advanced black churches did not permit these emerging artists to sing at their churches. However, as these artists grew in social status and were appreciated and accepted by the white culture, tolerance and approval gradually grew in black churches (Lincoln and Mamiya, 1990).

The research of Raymond Wise, Horace Boyer, and Eileen Southern covering the golden age of gospel is often referred to as the traditional period, from the 1940s to the1960s. Eric Lincoln and Lawrence H. Mamiya begin their study starting around the 1930s. Regardless of the exact date, the trend of gospel music during the mid-century years was influenced by the fact that this genre was not fully accepted in the mainline Black Church denominations, which contained the majority of black Christians. As a result, these emerging gospel artists leaned heavily toward establishing a new cultural space for their religious expression. In his research, Wise explains how this era demonstrated an increase in publishing, radio broadcasting, and recording and in concerts and performances by gospel artists outside the four walls of the traditional Black Church.

During this era the nation's oldest continuously running black-owned-and-operated publishing company for black gospel music was established. It was called Martin and Morris Music Company and was co-owned by Sallie Martin, formerly a soloist who had worked closely with Thomas Dorsey, and Kenneth Morris, a gospel music composer. Some resources show it as the Martin and Morris Studio. It was in operation from 1940 until the 1980s (Wise, 2002).

Their company and images of submitted material are documented in the National Archives of American History at the Smithsonian Institution. Martin and Morris served together in ministry at the First Church of Deliverance in Chicago, where Martin sang in the choir and Morris was the choir director. Sallie Martin was an established gospel artist who toured internationally with the Sallie Martin Singers. Her involvement with Thomas Dorsey helped promote and establish the gospel music genre. Morris, originally from New York, was a former professional jazz musician who had toured with his own jazz group for a period and eventually established himself in the gospel music community of Chicago (Smithsonian Institution, 2015). Kenneth Morris is accredited with introducing the Hammond organ to gospel music and was the author of well-known hymns like "Just a Closer Walk with Thee," "Yes, God Is Real," and "Christ Is All" (Wise, 2002).

Wise explains that this surge to publish gospel music brought along with it a learning curve of the music business. Many gospel artists did not copyright their music, simply because there was not a huge demand for purchasing gospel music. Reagon points out in *We'll Understand It Better By and By* that many gospel artists did not feel that obtaining a copyright was worth the money (Reagon, 1992). Wise explains that sheet music at this time sold for ten cents a copy, and the cost to copyright a song was two dollars. Unfortunately, Kenneth Morris served as an example of what could happen when a song does not have a copyright. He was the victim of music theft when "Just a Closer Walk with Thee" was stolen by a white publisher named Winsett. Morris did not have a copyright for it (Wise, 2002).

Wise (2002) explains that this incident made gospel composers realize that white-owned publishers now had interest in black gospel music. Obtaining a copyright became standard practice. By 1946, Southern white music stores began distributing black gospel sheet music. Martin and Morris would eventually establish 326 agents across the US, the West Indies, and England to help them operate their publishing company. Their clientele included James Cleveland, Alex Bradford, Dorothy Coates, Lucie Campbell, and Sam Cooke. The company's earnings would eventually reach $160,000 annually.

The golden age of gospel demonstrated exposure of gospel music not only through sheet music publishing but also through radio and recordings. Gospel music was propelled during weekly broadcasts and through gospel choirs. In the Chicago area, a well-known choir was Rev. Cobb and the First Church of Deliverance Radio Choir, which sang music written by Chicago-area gospel composers. Choirs across the nation would hear these broadcasts and replicate the musical style they heard from this choir and others like it. Wise mentions that blacks began purchasing gospel records after World War II and gained the attention of famous labels. Famous labels during the 1940s that started to record gospel music included Columbia, Savoy, Peacock, and Vee-Jay Records. These companies developed catalogues of gospel music and secured the future of gospel music in the recording industry (Wise, 2002).

It was also during this era that gospel music gained world recognition in non-traditional settings of the Black Church. Roberta Thorpe, the Golden Gate Jubilee Quartet, and the Dixie Hummingbirds performed gospel music in secular venues such as nightclubs and the Apollo Theater. Mahalia Jackson, a music colleague whose claim to fame was influenced by Dorsey, is accredited with bringing gospel music to international recognition. She toured Europe in 1952 and became the first international gospel artist when she sold one million copies of "Move On Up A Little Higher" in 1947. Additionally, Clara Ward and the Ward Singers, also discovered by Thomas Dorsey, toured internationally, singing in concert halls and theaters, in nightclubs, and on TV shows (Wise, 2002).

By the mid-1940s gospel music had become accepted in most black denominational churches. In 1948, Mahalia Jackson and Theodore Frye helped advance the acceptance in Baptist churches when they co-founded the National Baptist Music Convention. This was an auxiliary of the National Baptist Convention to train church musicians. This convention became a breeding ground for composers like Herbert Brewster. He wrote in the gospel blues tradition and in gospel ballad, recitative, and aria styles. These are slow storytelling musical forms and performed in the 12/8 gospel rhythm. He is noted for advancing gospel music theater with his song writing, including "Move On Up A Little Higher" and "Surely God Is Able." These songs sold one million copies and contributed to establishing Mahalia Jackson and the Clara Ward Singers on the national stage. He became head of the drama department for the convention and was known as the father of gospel music theater (Wise, 2002).

Gospel music beyond the Black Church was visible in the establishment of various entities. Community gospel choirs became popular. They were an outlet for those who loved gospel music and sought to sing a variety of styles. One such group established in 1948 in Chicago was the Thompson Community Singers, founded by Milton Brunson (Wise, 2002).

Ensembles and smaller groups like female groups, all-male quartet groups, duets, soloists, and mixed voice groups formed. Several contributors were trendsetters for this era. The Sallie Martin Singers sang three-part harmony of alto, lead, and innovatively added soprano coloratura. This set a tradition that would continue to be heard in choirs and groups. Rosetta Tharpe and Marie Knight sang as a female duet, and Roberta Martin was the first to mix female and male singers together in her group, the Roberta Martin Singers. The quartet groups began to demonstrate a more commercial appeal. They sang in suits and not robes and wore attire that had public appeal. The Jackson Southernaires and the Sensational Nightingales joined the ranks in 1940, along with prior established groups. Like secular artists, they encouraged crowd interaction and would aim for an emotional appeal to the audience. The Mighty Clouds of Joy were noted for being the first to introduce amplified instruments in their accompaniment in lead and bass guitars, as well as the keyboard. Drums were already in place (Wise, 2002).

In the 1950s, the expansion of gospel music across the country and the world was attributed to what was called "the gospel highway." This was a network of churches, schools, and arenas that became the venue where gospel artists were accepted and introduced and performed new music. The circuit enabled artists to easily travel and tour the country. The era of the golden age of gospel, 1945–1965, brought acceptance for gospel music as it became routine in black church services (Wise, 2002).

A sustainable gospel music industry was evident during this era with key milestones. Joe Bostic produced and promoted his first annual Gospel, Spirituals, and Folk Music Festival at Madison Square Garden, which included James Cleveland as a headliner. Mahalia Jackson's contributions were breakthroughs in that she had multiple revenue streams. She already had established the first million-seller gospel record in the 1940s when she appeared in films and on stages with secular artists like Louis Armstrong and Duke Ellington. She was the first gospel artist to be on *The Ed Sullivan Show* and the first to have her own network television show, *The Mahalia Jackson Show*. Her contracts with Columbia Records and CBS network paved the way for gospel music in the music and entertainment industry. She is considered the first legitimate gospel superstar (Wise, 2002).

Numerous gospel groups and artists achieved prominence during the golden age. A complete research project could be totally dedicated to their many individual contributions. To establish a comprehensive list would be a major undertaking, as many artists became well established regionally. Several trailblazers from this era laid the foundation for other well-established artists and groups as the gospel music industry began to unfold. Growth no longer depended on the church for sustainability. Albertina Walker established The Caravans in 1953, a national all-female group that appeared on major stages such as New York's Lincoln Theater and Madison Square Garden. Members changed over the years within The Caravans. Dorothy Norwood, Shirley Caesar, Inez Andrews, Cassietta George, Bessie Griffin, and Delores Washington eventually became established solo artists who would further contribute to the gospel music genre. Their male pianists over the years included Eddie Williams, James Herndon, and James Cleveland, before he became known for his legendary contributions (Wise, 2002).

The venue for gospel music continued to reach into secular audiences and mainstream music. Along with this came controversy over the role of the gospel artist in the mainstream music industry. Some artists saw this as an opportunity to minister to a wider audience while having incomes that fully sustained them. Others liked the entertainment edge and saw it as a way to pique a secular audience's interest in gospel music. There were those who were not attracted to glitz and glamor of the music business in mainstream industry and sought to stick to the gospel circuit (Wise, 2002).

For those who wanted to expand their options, the audience was now multi-racial and included popular culture. Gospel artists competed in the music and entertainment industry market like secular artists. Their look and presence became more commercialized, and their appeal grew for the church and mainstream secular venues. The gospel artist traded in their robes for elaborate dresses, appealing hairstyles, and the polished look of entertainers. Gospel artists began to focus on presentation and showmanship (Wise, 2002).

Some record labels were able to influence gospel artists to leave gospel music altogether and bring their gospel sound to R&B, blues, and jazz. However, numerous African-American singers had roots in the Black Church regardless of the genre they sought. Their church roots were reflected in any music they delivered (Wise, 2002).

The Staple Singers, established in 1953 in Chicago by Roebuck "Pop" Staples, was a family group that sang gospel quartet style. They eventually grew to prominence in the popular and mainstream music arenas. In their more than 50-year reign in the industry, their music style evolved from gospel-folk to funk to soul and eventually grew to a universal appeal. Their evolution allowed them to top the billboard charts with million-record sellers in the 1970s like "Respect Yourself" and "I'll Take You There." Their music was message oriented and inspirational. It paved the way for cross-over artists such as Kirk Franklin, Yolanda Adams, and BeBe and CeCe Winans. The Staple Singers were inducted into the Rock and Roll Hall of Fame in 1999. Their climb to fame paralleled the civil rights movement (Carpenter, 2005).

A discussion on this era would not be completed without mentioning the evolution of the gospel choir. The gospel choir was revolutionized by composers like Mattie Moss-Clark, James Cleveland, Jesse Dixon, Clay Evans, Doris Akers, Alex Bradford, and Raymond Rasperry, just to name a few. The contributions of Mattie Moss-Clark, along with the overall influence of the Church of God in Christ, were notable in her involvement in the Southwest Michigan State Choir. She would rise to recognition as a musician, choir director, and composer. Her style was emulated by numerous choirs across the nation. Her influence was heard in recordings from the 200-voice Southwest Michigan State Choir, established in 1959, and the 1,500-member Church of God in Christ Convocation Choir. She was the first to initiate and record a mixed choir that sang in three-part harmony. She would also later be known for introducing her daughters, the Clark Sisters, to the gospel music industry, planting a seed for their gospel music dynasty that continues until today (Wise, 2002).

James Cleveland was on the rise during the late 1950s and early 1960s for his singing and style of piano playing that connected him with various gospel groups in the Chicago area. His style was heavily influenced by Roberta Martin. Cleveland was also a former understudy of Dorsey and in 1959 established his own group called the Gospel Chimes. Cleveland eventually moved to Detroit for a minister of music position and would spread the sound of the traditional gospel choir wherever he went. He recorded with various gospel choirs and would eventually carry the baton as a drum major of gospel music influence (Wise, 2002).

Gospel musical *Black Nativity*, written by Langston Hughes, made a milestone in the gospel music industry as the first gospel musical to tour on both sides of the Atlantic Ocean. It provided another venue for gospel music, as it depicted Hughes's black interpretation of the birth of Christ (Southern, 1997).

Contemporary Period (Late 1960s–1970s)
(Note: 1967 to present often referred to as the Modern Contemporary Era)
Civil Rights Movement and Post-Civil Rights Era

In the late 1960s, gospel music expressed the souls of blacks and whites alike who were tired of the socioeconomic and political conditions that had plagued the opportunities of black Americans. It was black sacred music that encouraged enslaved Africans who had escaped to freedom on the Underground Railroad, who had awaited legal freedom by the Emancipation Proclamation, and who had lived through the Jim Crow laws of the South; to this point they had endured a lifestyle of separatism, segregation, and inequality. Although strides were being made for the gospel music genre as its artists graced world-renowned concert halls and theaters, these new "musical stars" were still black Americans off stage. Very few were afforded acceptance in this arena. This era of protest for civil rights and against the Vietnam War gave artists of all genres an opportunity to speak for the people through their lyrics. Songs spoke to the humanitarian perspective that would encourage the nation during a turbulent time. Freedom songs included favored hymns of the church and Negro spirituals like "Oh, Freedom!" "Woke Up This Morning with My Mind on Jesus," and "Love Lifted Me."

A popular theme song of the movement was "We Shall Overcome," an adaptation of Tindley's "I'll Overcome Someday." During the movement, Dr. King would call on the soulful voice of Mahalia Jackson to sing his favorite hymn, Dorsey's "Precious Lord, Take My Hand" (Castellini, 2013).

Well-established gospel composer and pastor Herbert Brewster was an active political force in Memphis, Tennessee, where he resided. At his church he wrote "Move On Up A Little Higher," which was popularized by Mahalia Jackson, to inspire the blacks of Memphis not to settle for less. Brewster's music was heard by then-truck driver Elvis Presley, who periodically visited East Trigg Baptist Church to hear their well-regarded gospel choir. Brewster was a colleague of Dr. King and had spoken with him the day he was assassinated (Castellini, 2013).

Rev. C. L. Franklin of Detroit was a radio disc jockey for gospel music and a well-known whooping preacher. He was also Aretha Franklin's father. Rev. Franklin established his national fame as a civil rights activist and sold recorded sermons on the issues of the movement. He and Mahalia Jackson organized a concert where she sang and raised $50,000 for the Birmingham campaign led by the Southern Christian Leadership Conference, SCLC (Castellini, 2013). Mahalia Jackson, who in 1961 sang for the inauguration of President John F. Kennedy, supported Dr. King with her prominence. She sang at the 1963 March on Washington, where Dr. King delivered his most famed speech, "I Have a Dream" (Wise, 2002).

The untimely death of King created an emptiness in the souls of black people. Aretha Franklin, who was had established herself as the queen of soul in the 1960s, consoled blacks at King's funeral when she sang "Precious Lord, Take My Hand."

Amidst the movement, the gospel music industry continued to thrive. Southern (1997) reports that *TV Gospel Time*, a 1963 television show dedicated to the gospel music genre, broadcasted in 60 major cities every Sunday morning. The Clara Ward singers continued to bring exposure to gospel music with their frequent appearances on famed shows like *The Flip Wilson Show, The Ed Sullivan Show* and *the Merv Griffin Show*. They became the first gospel group to sing at Radio City Music Hall. Ward also performed for President Lyndon B. Johnson. (Southern, 1997).

Key musical influences during the contemporary period were James Cleveland, Andréa Crouch, and Edward Hawkins. Some scholars refer to the period from 1967 to the current day as the modern contemporary era. The contributions of each of these are extensive and will only be summarized for this focus. James Cleveland, the first artist to introduce the concept of live recordings in 1963 with "Peace, Be Still," paved the way for other artists. Wise states that his lucrative contract with Savoy Records helped make Savoy Records the premier gospel label in the 1960s. This contract allowed him to discover, record, and produce hundreds of groups with Savoy Records. He also contributed to the success of various gospel choirs in the industry, such as the Angelic Choir, which sang "Peace, Be Still." His appeal came largely from his ability to compose simple call-and-response songs that told a story, stated a fact, and offered a resolution in a congregational gospel blues format. His ability to interact with the audience was notable. His practice of audience participation and manipulation allowed him to deliver the message of the song with an emotional connection. He often borrowed a secular phrase of a popular song and transformed it into a spiritual lyric. For example, he did this in "Jesus Is the Best Thing That Ever Happened to Me," a spin on "You're the Best Thing That Ever Happened to Me," by Gladys Knight and the Pips. His group, the Cleveland Singers, was well polished and groomed future artists such as Billy Preston, Kurt Karr, and Keith Pringle. Perhaps Cleveland's most impactful contribution was his establishment of the Gospel Music Workshop of America (GMWA) in 1969. It focused on improving standards of gospel music performance and aimed to develop the careers of gospel musicians. The organization was non-denominational and became an entry into the gospel music industry for aspiring gospel artists. Local chapters disseminated the teaching and practices until updates and new trends were introduced at the next annual convention meeting. GMWA became the largest national gospel organization in the world and helped validate Cleveland as the king of gospel music. The annual meeting grew to 20,000 delegates, who attended courses and participated in various guilds. GMWA linked the traditional artist and sound to the up-and-coming contemporary style of gospel (Wise, 2002).

Andraé Crouch brought a new sound to gospel music that included musical elements of popular music, rock, country, traditional gospel, and electronic instrumentation. His multi-racial group, the Disciples, appealed to black and white audiences. He appealed to young artists and would eventually establish a successful career in Christian and mainstream venues. Crouch recorded on Light Records and opened the door for numerous other artists through his producing. This included Walter Hawkins; his twin sister, Sandra Crouch; and the Winans (Wise, 2002).

A pivotal moment in gospel music was the unanticipated success of Edward Hawkins's rendition of "O Happy Day," released in 1969. He gained national recognition as the father of contemporary gospel music when he became the first to achieve this level in the realm of contemporary music. This rearranged hymn would take the gospel music industry to another level. It was the first recording in gospel music history to transcend genres and cross over to rock and roll, jazz, and folk music listeners. Sales reached over seven million copies, and Edward Hawkins received a Grammy Award for achieving chart position on the pop charts because of airplay on secular stations. The Hawkins Singers debuted the hit at Madison Square Garden and toured the US in venues that included nightclubs. As a result, their intent of ministry was called into question and was offensive to many black church members (Wise, 2002).

The Hawkins Singers consisted of the Hawkins Family, which had roots in the Church of God in Christ. Hawkins, like Crouch, fused the harmonic chords of popular music, blues, and jazz into this new gospel sound. Wise references Reagon and calls the Hawkins sound contemporary with a blend of classic gospel with Euroclassical and jazz ingredients. He introduced the practice of using sevenths, seconds, and dissonance tones in the instrumentation and vocal parts (Wise, 2002).

By the late 1960s and the 1970s, the number of blacks seeking higher education exposed a new generation to formal training in various types of African-American and European classical sacred music. As early as 1961, a forerunner in the integration of classical music influence into gospel was Clinton Utterbach and his Utterbach Concert Ensemble. He introduced a "swing" style of playing the pipe organ and the gospel anthem. This style of singing was partially narrated and partially sung. Many of his arrangements have been used by black and white composers alike.

Black gospel musicians who were formally trained like Utterbach found out that in academic settings, performance of gospel was forbidden because it was not seen as aesthetically acceptable. Classically trained gospel musicians were discouraged from continuing gospel music in college music department events at HBCUs. Black college students began to organize and operate gospel choirs, sometimes independently and without assistance from their universities. Richard Smallwood was among the organizers of the Howard University Gospel Choir in 1965, starting a trend at other colleges and universities. This exposure would eventually reveal itself not only in academic settings but also in the musical styles of composers in the community and the gospel music industry (Wise, 2002).

In the 1970s, traditional gospel music flourished. Familiar artists on the scene included the phenomenal Shirley Caesar, known as the first lady of gospel. She was eventually called the queen of gospel as she evangelized in her music. Others during this decade included Milton Brunson, Mattie Moss Clark, Alex Bradford, and Albertina Walker. During this same time, James Cleveland and Aretha Franklin collaborated on a series of recordings. Traditional quartet groups like the Jackson Southernaires and the Dixie Hummingbirds were still mainstream groups. Female quartet groups on the scene included the Truthettes and the Steele Family (Wise, 2002).

The sound evolved with a new music vocabulary and expansion in instrumentation and now classical influence from artists like Richard Smallwood and the Richard Smallwood Singers. Classically trained choir directors influenced the sophistication of gospel college choirs. In 1972, the formation of the National Black Gospel College Choir Workshop became a forum for practitioners. Bowling Green State University Gospel Choir was one of the first college gospel choirs to record and gain national recognition as a recording choir (Wise, 2002).

The Hawkins Family reigned as a musical dynasty in the 1970s. The five recordings of "Love Alive" by Walter Hawkins and the Love Center Church Choir demonstrated the next generation of harmonic vocabulary for gospel music, vocals, and instrumentation. Their music brought innovation in orchestration and in solo work, as demonstrated by the recordings of Tramaine Hawkins (Wise, 2002).

In 1979, Edwin Hawkins established a new gospel music workshop called the Edwin Hawkins Music and Arts Seminar. The first session was held in San Francisco. It was established after Edwin realized the lack of valid information on the history and development of black religious music, especially modern-day contemporary gospel and its place as an art form. Hawkins noted that the use of sacred dance and drama as a conveyor of the spirit and culture of blacks was not being taught as an academic discipline. This convention was established to close this gap and to teach this diverse perspective of music in development.

Later in 1988, Walter Hawkins would lead an effort of Atlanta pastors in the establishment of the Love Fellowship Convention. It provided pastors and their congregations the opportunity to refresh their spirits through joint praise, worship, and education without regard to denominational affiliations. In 1994, as explained on the conference website, Edwin Hawkins and Walter Hawkins combined their efforts. This convention has continued to offer the highest level of professional instruction in culturally relevant areas of Christian music, dance, and drama. In addition to true Christian fellowship, it has become a highlight activity for many churches worldwide. The conference has since been renamed the Edwin Hawkins and Walter Hawkins Music & Arts Love Fellowship Conference (Hawkins Gospel Conference, 2015).

White record labels Light Records and Sparrow Records capitalized on black gospel music. They also published songbooks for these recordings that were purchased by a musically literate audience and church musicians. The resurgence in demand for sheet music, which had toppled in the 1960s upon the invention of the photocopy machine, enabled Kenneth Morris to regain a presence in publications. Now the owner of Morris Music Company (after buying out Martin's portion), he distributed music for artists, including Andrea Couch, Edwin Hawkins, Walter Hawkins, Sandi Patti, and Bill Gaither. A new practice of releasing compilation CDs contained the most popular hits of a series of artists on the same label. This practice came into existence as a result of competition between traditional and contemporary gospel record companies (Wise, 2002).

The late 1970s captured several new major milestones in gospel music that would have industry influence. Gospel music was not only in black Baptist, Methodist, and Pentecostal denominations; it also traversed into black Catholic, Episcopal, and Presbyterian churches. A wider Black Church audience was incorporating gospel into worship services (Wise, 2002).

In 1976, the *New National Baptist Hymnal* was published. It included selections from Tindley, Dorsey, and other gospel trailblazers. It was adapted as the hymnal for various denominations and continues in wide use today (Wise, 2002).

Wise (2002) notes that *The Bobby Jones Show* launched on television in 1976 as the first nationally syndicated gospel television show on Black Entertainment Television (BET). This show was to gospel music what *Soul Train* was to R&B and soul music. *The Bobby Jones Show* helped launch the careers of gospel artists by providing them with exposure and introducing their music to the international gospel community. The show eventually aired on other networks and became the longest-running show on cable TV. Bobby Jones recently announced their 35th and final season (BET, 2015).

Andraé Crouch helped enable the wider audience appeal that occurred with gospel music in the 1970s. He is accredited with incubating the word/ministry movement in which words would become the differentiating factor of gospel music. Although Crouch contributed to the change in musical style and more versatility, the message would not be compromised. Crouch appealed to a multicultural audience, not just to African-Americans. This trait was a leading indicator for what would evolve to become the Christian contemporary genre. This is the mainstream genre for white gospel popular music.

Wise (2002) quotes Southern's (1997) account of the strides gospel music has made since its entry on the black sacred music scene, starting with the Dorsey era. These factors demonstrate it as a sustainable industry and art form: 1) It was an established genre internationally. 2) The venues where gospel music was heard included churches of all denominations, college campuses with sizable black student populations, and mainstream public venues like concert halls, theaters, some nightclubs, radio, and television. 3) It was produced in quantity by record labels. 4) Gospel literature was researched in academia and in intellectual circles and documented in articles, discography, and doctoral dissertations. 5) National workshops were available for training on practices and acceptable standards of performance, sharing new material, providing exposure for new compositions, and preserving black traditions.

Modern Contemporary (late 1960s–1970s/1980s– 1990)
Emerging Trends in Gospel

The 1980s was a time when the gospel music industry grew, and the categories of black music genres expanded to include gospel, soul, pop, and spirituals as the number of gospel record companies increased. Two of the key labels of this era were Onyx Records (Richard Smallwood, Vanessa Bell, and Thomas Whitfield), Rejoice Records (Shirley Caesar, Douglas Miller, Albertina Walker, Tramaine Hawkins, The Clark Sisters, The Mighty Clouds of Joy, Milton Brunson, and the Thompson Community Singers). Wise reports that black artists were not often treated fairly by these major labels. Cleveland decided to start King James Records (1985) to provide artists with more involvement in all aspects of recording. The artists on this label included The GMWA Mass Choir, James Cleveland, Cleveland Singers, and Billy Preston, to name a few.

Gospel music gained even more exposure through nationally syndicated radio, TV, and print media. Chicago, the birth city of gospel music, had a series of events in 1980 called *The Golden Jubilee of Gospel*, culminating in a pageant called *The Roots of Gospel*. In 1983, Burke Johnson hosted *Inspirations Across America*, a nationally syndicated radio show that reviewed a countdown of inspirational hits. Television airwaves broadcasted *God Sound* in Detroit, with host Darryl Ford and Wintley Phipps hosting the *Stellar Showcase. Bobby Jones Gospel Music Review* increased their show time from 30 to 60 minutes. A landmark documentary called *Say Amen, Somebody,* explored the growth of gospel music in America. It included classic footage of interviews and conversations with Thomas Dorsey, Sallie Martin, and Willie Mae Ford Smith. In 1980, print media launched *Totally Gospel Magazine*, published by T. J. Hemphill. *Score Magazine* (later called *Gospel Today*) was published by Teresa Hairston.

Another major trend in gospel music in the 1980s was the sophistication in touring and concerts. The production quality of gospel concerts took on the form normally associated with secular music, including lighting, special effects, big stadium sound, and choreography. The artists hired additional musicians and vocalists for improved orchestration for live music that was as good as or even better than the recordings. Gospel artists were no longer just groups singing at church concerts. Their entourages included production staffs. A team generally consisted of a sound technician, lighting/special effects technician, road manager, business manager, stage manager, background vocalists, rhythm/orchestral musicians, wardrobe/uniform coordinator, hair stylist, makeup artist, transportation/lodging personnel, and sales staff. Honorarium rates would no longer cover the cost of the touring gospel artist. Tickets prices increased to cover these costs and allow for a profit for living expenses. National artists hired professional management companies and no longer managed themselves (Wise, 2002).

Major artists who operated at this level included Andraé Crouch, the Hawkins Family, and new to the national scene, the Winans and Commissioned. The Winans and Commissioned, both based in Detroit, brought a new branding and more contemporary gospel sound to gospel music (Wise, 2002).

The Winans, a contemporary all-male quartet group of brothers, debuted in 1981 with an album produced by Andraé Crouch on Light Records called *The Question Is*. The Winans would become a major force in gospel music in the 1980s, with a total of eight albums in the 1980s and other releases in the upcoming decades that would have crossover appeal (All Music, 2015). The Winans family was a gospel music dynasty that included the parents, Mom and Pop Winans, and several groups, duos, and solo releases from the children. This includes duos BeBe and CeCe and younger siblings Debbie and Angie. The Winan brothers are Carvin, Marvin, Ron, Michael, David (instrumentalist), and Daniel (All Music, 2015).

Commissioned, an all-male contemporary gospel group, was known for its high-tech productions and rock-style concerts that had an evangelistic approach. The concerts would offer an altar call to the audience for repentance. The group formed in 1984 and would reign until the 2000s. Several members—Fred Hammond, Marvin Sapp, Keith Staten, and Michael Brooks—pursued successful solo careers. Commissioned released four albums in the 1980s and went on to produce a series of releases in the following decades (All Music, 2015).

In the 1980s, large corporations began to recognize the influence of gospel music on black consumers. Gospel music festivals and competition were new venues for exposure of gospel music. Nationally known events were sponsored by McDonald's, Kentucky Fried Chicken, Quaker Oats, and Wrigley's Chewing Gum. These events were to demonstrate the corporate sponsors' commitment to the African-American community, which provided consumer dollars, and to African-American franchise owners and employees (Wise, 2002).

Black gospel artists were not as popular among the general public because their labels spent less marketing money for them than for white artists. Also, secular artists with gospel roots could record a gospel album, and their popularity would position them for Grammy Awards ahead of those artists consistently committed to it. There was also discontent due to the omitted gospel music segment from the televised Grammy Awards (Wise, 2002).

The concerns of these artists were raised to organizations that sponsored prestigious music awards. As a result, gospel musicians began getting recognized by these entities for their contributions to gospel music and entertainment in general. The Gospel Music Hall of Fame, which focused on the white-targeted Christian Contemporary genre, inducted Thomas Dorsey in 1982 as the first African-American recipient. In 1981, James Cleveland becomes the first gospel artist inducted to the Hollywood Walk of Fame (Wise, 2002).

Totally Gospel Magazine introduced a Reader Poll Award, and GMWA launched the Gospel Music Excellence Awards in the early 1980s. These efforts provided recognition of black gospel artists among the black listening audience. In 1985, Don Jackson launched the Stellar Awards, a prestigious televised gala dedicated to the achievements of black gospel artists. Qualifications for nominees were patterned from the Grammy Awards and recipient selection based on record sales, chart listings, and private and public voting bodies (Wise, 2002).

Scholarly studies of gospel music were on the rise in the 1980s, including Bernice Reagon's *We'll Understand It By and By*. She also hosted a radio program as a joint venture with the Smithsonian Institution and National Public Radio. A collection of broadcasts that covered the history of gospel music was compiled into a cassette series called *Wade in the Water*. Additionally, various denominations released new hymnals featuring the works of gospel pioneers. These include *Songs of Zion* in 1981 (United Methodist), *Lift Every Voice and Sing* in 1981 (the Episcopal Church), and *Yes, Lord* in 1985 (the Church of God in Christ) (Wise, 2002).

A variety of gospel artists, traditional and contemporary, thrived during the 1980s. Contemporary groups on the rise included Chicago-based Milton Brunson and the Thompson Community Singers (also known as "The Tommie"). They released the first of a series of albums called *Available to You*. The Tommies would become a reigning choir for a decade's worth of releases and gospel music impact. Additionally, the Richard Smallwood Singers made their debut in 1982 and presented a polished style and classic hits. They released choir standards such as "I Love the Lord" and "Jesus, You're the Center of My Joy." Traditional artists Shirley Caesar and James Cleveland maintained relevance by incorporating a contemporary style of music with their traditional singing. Quartet groups like the Williams Brothers were also innovative in seeking a contemporary flavor (Wise, 2002).

Wise points out that a new musical movement occurred. Contemporary gospel music was now accepted in non-traditional denominations. R&B, rap, and hip-hop elements were being incorporated into traditional and contemporary music. This was demonstrated by artists such as Andraé Crouch, the Clark Sisters, John P. Kee, Take 6, and Tramaine Hawkins. There was continued focus on the words of the song and less on the musical style. Urban contemporary was incubated with seeds planted by Andraé Crouch, the Winans, and Commissioned. Their contemporary sound attracted young people for a ministry purpose. This practice was unpopular with large secular record companies. They wanted artists to stop altar calls in the concerts, asking them to compromise the gospel message (Wise, 2002).

An exhaustive list of influential artists of varied styles made contributions during the 1980s. A few of these trailblazers were John P. Kee, Hezekiah Walker, Thomas Whitfield, Vanessa Bell Armstrong, and Daryl Coley, who all blended R&B, soul, funk, or jazz in their styles. Kee, Walker, Bell, and Coley demonstrated a new style in solo singing that was a more improvised, ornamented, and virtuoso style of singing. It was attractive to the new generation. Kee and Walker organized community choirs that had strong urban appeal and ministered to the challenges that plagued black youth (Wise, 2002).

Hip-hop and rap music were strong on the secular scene and by the 1980s were influencing gospel music. A forerunner in this area was Harvard-educated Pastor Rev. Dr. Dexter Wise, who was called to minister at the age of 12 and licensed at the age of 19. When he entered the gospel music industry with his release "I Ain't Into That," Dr. Wise was pastoring Shiloh Baptist Church in Columbia, Ohio. Wise is the brother of gospel music scholar Dr. Raymond Wise, whose work has been valuable in tracing the history of gospel music. Dr. Wise assisted in producing "I Ain't Into That," which charted in major cities in the US and internationally in the UK. He saw rap as a way to package the gospel to reach the youth of the era. Infusing rap and hip-hop music into gospel music was not a widely accepted practice at the time but paved the way for Christian rap/hip-hop (Wise, 2002).

Whitfield, Tankard, and Allen and Allen introduced the gospel jazz style and even instrumental gospel music, setting the stage for more gospel jazz artists. Their contributions would eventually aid in the establishment of new categories at gospel awards ceremonies (Wise, 2002).

The next musical movement Wise discusses is a Word-based movement focusing on evangelism and transformation called praise and worship. It appealed to megachurches and Word-based ministries. It appealed to a new generation of young people, including African-Americans who were not familiar with a church experience. Blacks migrated to white Word churches in search of a spiritual and intellectually geared worship experience. Initially, praise and worship yielded from the attraction of both black and white Christians to Word churches. It was aesthetically and culturally neutral and did not take root in the Black Church until mega Word churches began to grow in the black church community. Praise and worship was an adaptation of the congregational and devotional singing that African-Americans had practiced in worship in the 19th and early 20th centuries. This was before choirs became standard in the Black Church. There was no specific genre for what seemed to be the norm for the Black Church. The praise and worship genre was primarily developed in the Christian music industry by white artists. Black artists such as Donnie McClurkin and Patrick Henderson recognized the contribution of early black congregations and compiled praise and worship medleys from the black church devotional style of worship (Wise, 2002).

Contemporary Period (1990s–2000)
Emerging Trends in Gospel Music Business and Sound

Wise (2002) discusses the urban influence of gospel music in the last decade of the 20th century. Gospel music had the attention of major record labels that focused on the profitability and possibilities it offered from a commercial standpoint. This movement of major labels to gospel music brought pros and cons to the artists. Pros included the following: 1) The quality of the gospel music recording was competitive with other genres. 2) Gospel music gained widespread exposure as these labels used new strategic marketing approaches. (This will be discussed in further detail in this section.) 3) The rise in sales was attributed to changing demographics of the gospel music consumer. The audience for gospel music was no longer primarily in the Black Church. Gospel music was appreciated beyond the Black Church and gained the attention of mainstream popular culture.

As gospel artists joined major labels, cons included the following: 1) These labels gained economic control and dictated trends and practices in the gospel music industry. Prior to this time, the key contributors, pioneers, and organizations in gospel music formed the circle of influence that deployed change and introduced trends in gospel music. 2) Record labels driven by the profit of gospel music and not the prophecy of the gospel sought to secularize the artists to provide them with more crossover appeal. In doing so, they sought an image that minimized spirituality and the distinguishing traits of ministry. This included requiring artists to use generic words such as *love, light,* and *He* instead of directly stating *God, Jesus,* or the *Spirit* in the text of the music. 3) These new trends caused the traditional gospel audience to disconnect from artists who followed these guidelines. Thus, gospel artists left the major labels in pursuit of regaining independence. Black label executives and artists sought to establish their own independent labels, allowing them to benefit more from the profit. Major labels offered deals that provided artists with small percentages of profit, loss of publishing rights, and royalties in exchange for their services as a label (Wise, 2002).

Resulting from this chain of events, those artists who left the major labels still benefited indirectly from the overall increased exposure of gospel music in new venues. During this decade gospel music gained more opportunities for exposure through strategic marketing approaches from the major record labels. As it competed with secular music, the major record labels provided increased exposure to gospel music through increased radio airplay, television, and print media. This included airing videos in secular venues such as MTV and VH1. Video airplay was created in the gospel music space on BET when Bobby Jones launched *Video Gospel*. The new urban and crossover sound gave gospel music mainstream radio exposure. Syndicated radio and television shows dedicated to gospel music increased and 24-hour gospel radio stations emerged. Local and national gospel television shows became popular and provided gospel artists more opportunities for exposure. Established and major artists were often invited to appear on mainstream television network shows such as *The Tonight Show, Jay Leno,* and *The David Letterman Show* (Wise, 2002).

The increase in smaller independent labels oversaturated the gospel music industry market, diminishing the number of artists whose songs would receive radio airplay. A solution was to reapply the compilation CD concept. This allowed a legal approach for consumers to obtain the top gospel hits from various artists. This series of CDs was called *WOW Gospel*. The top hits of specific subgenres were included (Wise, 2002).

Collaborative recordings in gospel occurred that involved artists and producers working together from gospel and secular genres. Wise discusses extensively *The Messiah: A Soulful Celebration* as a major milestone. This project was produced by Mervyn Warren, who entered the music industry when he sang with the group Take 6. Warren provided a rendition of Handel's *Messiah,* which appealed to African-American worshipers. Those who participated in the collaboration included Tramaine Hawkins, Sound of Blackness, Richard Smallwood, Vanessa Bell, Daryl Coley, Chris Willis, George Duke, Al Jarreau, Tevin Baker, and Patti Austin. Quincy Jones conducted the "Hallelujah Chorus." This work demonstrated a classical influence in gospel music (Wise, 2002).

Warren's collaboration skills and classical influence were also demonstrated in the musical prelude "Total Praise," by Richard Smallwood, another pioneering maestro with classical influence. He helped expose gospel music on mainstream popular culture film with the collaborative work on the soundtrack for *Sister Act II*. Warren resurfaced "O Happy Day," and "Joyful, Joyful," with a cross-cultural and cross-generation appeal. Warren also worked on the soundtrack to *The Preacher's Wife* and arranged selections for popular secular artist Whitney Houston, who had church roots, and traditional artists the Georgia Mass Choir (Wise, 2002).

Another "pro" aspect or justification for going to major record labels was the access to or coexistence with media companies under the same ownership. This allowed them control in a positive light that exposed gospel artists and their music in major main stream media such as the *Prince of Egypt*. This collaborative effort involved a host of secular and gospel artists including Shirley Caesar, Fred Hammond, Boyz to Men, Kirk Franklin, Take 6, Donnie McClurkin, BeBe and CeCe Winans, Brian McKnight, Mary and Mary and Ty Tribbett, and GA (Wise, 2002).

By the late 1990s the thriving gospel music industry had organizations, conventions, and trade magazines to help propel it forward, provide forums for training and development, and gain recognition of achievements. Gospel artists could voice their concerns about unfair business practices from record labels to organizations like the United Gospel Industry Council. Protests were led by Frank Wilson in 1994. Wilson would become an advocate for just and fairness for gospel music and its artists (Wise, 2002).

Additionally, trade magazines that launched in the late 1990s were useful in documenting, archiving, and communicating accomplishments in gospel music. These included *The Gospel Industry Magazine, The Gospel Round Up,* and *Gospel Today,* formerly known as *Score Magazine.* Wise also includes *Gospel International, Gospel Industry Today, Gospel Northwest Magazine, Say Amen,* and *Billboard Online.* Record label executive Kerry Douglas launched *The Gospel Truth* to bring exposure to independent record labels and new artists. He focused heavily on quartet music (Wise, 2002).

The National Convention of Gospel Choirs and Choruses (NCGCC), founded by Thomas Dorsey, and The Gospel Music Workshop of America (GMWA), founded by James Cleveland, continued to be the premier training institutions in the gospel music industry. Other artists began launching seminars, workshops, conferences, and related organizations to provide places for training and curriculums for learning. Gospel music and black sacred music could also be studied academically (Wise, 2002).

Wise (2002) focuses on several artists of the 1990s who were groundbreaking and made extensive, innovative, and in-depth contributions to gospel music. By this time the growth of gospel music was enormous. The life work of each of the many impactful artists during the 1990s deserves an academic synthesis.

John P. Kee is recognized for his contributions and incubation of the hip-hop gospel movement in the 1980s. Kee's music offered contemporary, funk, R&B flavor, and traditional vocals. John P. Kee and his choir called New Life Community Choir appealed to the youth and young adult crowd in style and music. Kee's music could be replicated by church choirs for their repertoire. It was also available in score for those musicians and directors who were musically literate. His top releases included "Show Up" and "Strength" on Verity Records (Wise, 2002).

Hezekiah Walker and the Love Fellowship Crusade Choir were also known for their urban appeal. Walker's music was a major contributor to the urban contemporary choir movement. Walker was known for his easily chanted style songs that caught the attention of many youth. Examples include "Clean Inside" and "We've Got the Victory." His music was in a style that appealed to church choirs, as it was generally replicable for them (Wise, 2002).

Jimmy Jam and Terry Lewis, major producers of the R&B genre, produced a choir called Sounds of Blackness, which evolved from the 1968 McCallister College Choir. Their style originally focused on freedom songs and spirituals. When their director, Gary Hines, decided to expand their repertoire, the name changed to Sounds of Blackness. "Hold On, A Change Is Coming" was a major hit for Sounds of Blackness and brought them into the fold of other choirs recognized as a part of the urban choir movement (Wise, 2002).

Kirk Franklin became popular in 1993 after his album release *The Reason Why We Sing* brought him prominence and accolades that would eventually enable him to revolutionize the gospel music industry. Franklin's success would blossom the label and make him a major player in the music and entertainment industry (Wise, 2002).

Kirk Franklin and the Family released "The Reason Why We Sing" in 1993. By 1994, this was the number-two song of the year. At the Ninth Annual Stellar Awards, Kirk Franklin would be recognized as the "Best New Artist" and awarded with the "Song of the Year" recognition. It seemed that every record he touched charted with success. On the other hand, he became a controversial figure from the industry success he obtained from crossover hits. The controversy over his music overshadowed many of Franklin's great compositions in his albums that did not receive as much attention. He also had to sort through a series of legal issues resulting from those who felt slighted financially by his success. Kirk Franklin's contributions are discussed in further detail in an upcoming section of this work (Wise, 2002).

Fred Hammond (already known to the gospel scene as a former lead singer for Commissioned) and Radical for Christ continued the word and ministry-based approach that had been a trait of Commissioned. His music also contributed to the urban contemporary style, with emphasis on his skillful bass playing, yet his focus on the message continued to attract the traditional consumer base (Wise, 2002).

The review by Wise (2002) recognizes a trend in an urban appeal in gospel music. The discussion within the gospel music community was that this appeal was secularization that created ambiguity of what had once distinguished the gospel artists. It produced more financial gains but was controversial in the Black Church. The look and sound of the artists, their lyrical content, stage dances, appearance in secular venues, and even activities off stage were questioned by gospel music lovers and some fellow artists. Their style appealed to a young generation, yet to their traditional audience it seemed to be a compromise of the original intent of the gospel message. The controversial artists included Kirk Franklin, Mary Mary, and Trin-I-Tee 5:7, just to name a few.

The distinction between contemporary and traditional music was no longer enough to categorize gospel music. The debate on what was gospel and what was not helped to define more categorization: traditional gospel, contemporary gospel, urban contemporary, contemporary Christian (predominantly white audience), inspirational, new traditional, and praise and worship. Having these categories also provided a target focus for artists to decide on a category that was the best fit for their contributions (Wise, 2002).

This trend also provided new opportunities for more gospel artists to have cross-cultural appeal and even provided space for secular artists to record gospel. It was no longer just for the black churchgoers. Artists such as CeCe Winans and Anointed gained a large support base in the Christian contemporary genre. There was also a movement of secular artists who recorded gospel music. These included Oleta Adams, Helen Baylor, Aaron Neville, Brian McKnight, and Gladys Knight (Wise, 2002).

Gospel music had a style that had cross-cultural appeal as white congregations sought to have contemporary or charismatic worship. White artists who sang Christian contemporary began to record in a style that appealed to African-American worshipers. These included Angelo and Veronica, Crystal Lewis, and The Brooklyn Tabernacle Choir (Wise, 2002).

Numerous artists would gain prominence in the late 1990s and have sustained careers or pioneer trends into the new millennium. The list is extensive and the contributions of many of them could each be a stand-alone research project. A few examples include Donald Lawrence and The Tri-City Singers, Kurt Karr, Richard Smallwood, The Thompson Community Singers, William Becton and Friends, Ricky Dillard and New Generation Chorale, the

Wilmington Chester Mass Choir, and the Mississippi Choir. Each of these and a host of others brought lasting contributions and innovations. The full breadth of contributions from the numerous artists at this point is yet to be seen (Wise, 2002).

By the end of the 20th century, gospel music had grown to a complex organism that was more than just a soul-stirring song or a thriving industry. It was a business contender on the Billboard charts. Gospel music was a culture, an art form, an academic curriculum, a profession, and last but not least, the message of the good news through song.

Gospel Music in the New Millennium (2000–2015)

Raymond Wise (2002) explains that in the new millennium gospel music is one of the fastest-growing musical genres in the nation and the sixth most popular style of music. His research goes up to 2000 when its position was just behind rock, country, urban contemporary, pop, and rap. Gospel music had expanded into mainstream culture and markets. By this time, gospel music was receiving attention and promotion by secular artists, movies, and labels alike. It was not unusual to hear gospel music in rotation on mainstream radio. Industry professionals such as Lisa Collins, publisher of *Gospel Music Industry Round-Up*, accredit the innovative musical styles and practices of Kirk Franklin for the breakthrough growth of gospel music by 2000.

The worship space for gospel music was now definitely beyond the Black Church. This was primarily due to the popularity of the urban contemporary style of gospel, which was a by-product of marketing practices of major record labels that began to sign and promote gospel artists. Although this style was the most accepted in mainstream markets, high-volume record sales were also seen in traditional gospel music markets. Less profit was generated in traditional markets due to the smaller size. As a result, traditional gospel artists who were now living legends of the art form would not receive as much financial reward as those other genres (Wise, 2002).

The debate on the boundary lines of gospel music continued into the new millennium. The traditional gospel artists and audience struggled with the current musical sound of the day. There was little distinction in the instrumentation, chord structure, and composition from secular music. The controversial direction attracted new listeners outside the church, yet the question remained as to whether the purpose of the gospel message would be fulfilled. Would it appear as just entertainment to the non-Christian? Traditional artists who sought to stay current and relevant included Shirley Caesar, Dorothy Norwood, Albertina Walker, and various quartet groups. They made musical adaptations yet kept the traditional vocal style (Wise, 2002).

Gospel music from the early pioneers would be reinvented by contemporary artists to fit the new generation and musical trend. History would repeat itself in that those controversial practices in gospel music would eventually become the norm. This had been the case with Tindley, Dorsey, Morris, and Thorpe in the transitional era (1920s–1930s) before gospel music was accepted in all black churches. This was the same with artists like Andraé Crouch, The Hawkins Family, and the Clark Sisters in the contemporary years. Many of these artists were before their time—they were trailblazing the next standard for the genre (Wise, 2002).

Interview with Bob Marovich on the new millennium era, 2000–2015. Robert "Bob" Marovich, a black sacred music historian based in Chicago, traces and follows the history of gospel music. His website, *Journal of Gospel Music*, houses interviews with many past and present gospel artists and contains his publications. It also provides notice of speaking engagements where he makes others aware of the contributions of African-Americans in sacred music. He follows gospel music daily and journals an account of what is happening on the national landscape and how it impacts the African-American Christian worship community. Marovich is a radio announcer and recently published the book *A City Called Heaven*, which provides an account of gospel music's roots in Chicago. In this interview, Marovich commented on a summary of the major milestones and trends in gospel music from 2000 to 2015.

Marovich explained that the first major milestone in a synopsis of gospel music in the new millennium was the incorporation of praise and worship music into the service. He stated that this is philosophically the same concept and approach as the original change in the church in the pre-gospel era circa 1900. Tent revivalists of the second awakening sought simple songs, less complicated than hymns. The praise and worship songs serve the same purpose for both blacks and whites as the creation of gospel songs and hymns had served for blacks. Churches sought to return the congregation to participating in the service, thus taking music from the choir. As a result, a series of praise and worship artists entered the Contemporary Christian Music (CCM) genre. Their listeners are predominantly white. Black gospel artists began to reinvent and rework songs already released by white artists. They soon began getting awards for doing praise and worship music. This change has helped unify Christians across the cultural divide in the church (Marovich, 2015).

Bob Marovich noted that the second major movement that has occurred during the new millennium in the genre of gospel music is the movement of hip-hop. He referred to these artists as street evangelists and theologians of a new breed. Marovich has interviewed various rap artists, and he respects their humility as Christians and artists. They have multicultural appeal that is mainly attractive to the youth. Their music also is infiltrating mainstream hip-hop and reaches unchurched youth (Marovich, 2015).

The third movement he noted was an effort to resurface the choir in the church. However, the challenge is that artists are not releasing music the average church choir can sing. Expositions and competitions like *How Sweet the Sound* are venues to help the choir stay visible. Choirs are costly to operate and move at an industry level; thus, ensembles have been a feasible option that allows a big sound without the cost of transporting for touring (Marovich, 2015).

Marovich had several observations of gospel music from 2000 to 2015 and its outlook. He included these in his closing comments of the interview:

> It has always been the youth that moved gospel music to the next level. The use of YouTube can allow exposure to older music. The young generation can re-invent styles and groups of the past. As we become more of a global society, we see more global music in gospel, (and) sounds from other countries. This is the age for a new gospel super star to be birthed, someone like a Shirley Caesar, as the new king or queen of gospel. We are in a position for a changing-of-the-guard in all elements of gospel—that is, in singing, producing, and media. This will be someone who has an amazing effect on gospel.

Marovich noted potential in Le'Andria Johnson, Crystal Rucker, Dominique Jones, and Cathy Taylor to "reign" as the next queen of gospel. He did not mention any possible vocalist as the next king of gospel. He mentioned Lonny Hunter as possibly taking on the role of Bobby Jones, who has fostered talent on TV for 35 years. In 2015, he announced it would be the last season for the *Bobby Jones Gospel Show* on BET to air. Bobby Jones has been to gospel music what *Soul Train's* Don Cornelius provided to R&B and Soul and *American Bandstand's* Casey Kasem provided to pop and rock and roll music. The *Bobby Jones Gospel Show* was a pit stop that fueled the career for up-and-coming gospel artists who are established in the gospel music industry today (Marovich, 2015).

A Synopsis of 2000–2015 trailblazers. The new millennium displays adaptations in the evolution of gospel music and the African-American worship experience that share a trend in two main areas: 1) unleashing of limitations of gospel music and the artist in musical style, appeal, and branding; 2) music that bridges the sacred and secular realms. The artists included in this section are trailblazers or icons in the milestones noted by Bob Marovich. Additionally, their approach exemplifies the underlying themes of "unleashing of limitations" and "bridging sacred and secular," whose leading indicator before acceptance is controversial.

Contributions of Kirk Franklin in the new millennium. Kirk Franklin carried the torch for gospel music into the new millennium, leading the way for its creation for the age of hip-hop and urban soul (Turner, 2010). Franklin revolutionized the sound of gospel music and broke the chains that had confined it to limited exposure and limited appeal. Franklin further contemporized the "choir sound" with the ensemble approach already common in the gospel music industry. His controversial hit "Stomp" would join the ranks as another iconic and trendsetting gospel release, launching the era of streetwise urban spiritual music that is a blend of gospel, funk, hip-hop, and R&B. This hit, sung by his group, God's Property, represented Franklin's innovative approach to gospel music. The urban sound was coupled with lyrics that spoke to real issues faced by youth and young adults (Turner, 2010).

Kirk Dewayne Franklin came from humble beginnings. He was raised by his great-aunt Gertrude, who took him in as an abandoned child. On a limited income she enrolled him in piano lessons when he was four and recycled aluminum cans to cover the expense. She reared him with a strict Christian upbringing, and he became the music director of Mt. Rose Baptist Church adult choir, in Fort Worth, Texas, at the age of 12. As a teenager Kirk continued to display promising talent; at the same time he displayed behavioral problems in school. He suffered abuse by his stepfather and eventually fathered a child as a teenager. His erratic behavior included drug use, sexual promiscuity, and pornography addition. His moment of conversion occurred when a close friend was fatally shot. This wake-up call made him decide to return to the church and focus on composing gospel music. Through it all, his love for music was a constant connection to the church (All Music, 2015).

Franklin began to plant seeds for the music industry by seeking exposure to major artists who came to town. After gospel legend Milton Biggham heard one of his early compositions with his first group, the Humble Hearts, Biggham connected him with the Dallas-Fort Worth Mass Choir. They recorded a song he wrote called "Every Day with Jesus." Biggham continued to be impressed by Franklin's talents. When Franklin was 20, Milton Biggham hired him to direct the choir at the 1990 Gospel Music Workshop of America (GMWA) Convention in Washington, DC (All Music, 2015).

Franklin's reputation as a composer and choir director was boosted following his invitation to direct at the GMWA. In 1991, Kirk Franklin compiled an ensemble of 17 of his singing friends and colleagues called the Family. He compiled a demo of ten of his compositions and distributed it to national artists who came to town and mailed it to record labels. For the most part, the songs were traditional in nature. Among those he spoke with in the music business and the gospel music industry were BeBe Winans and Daryl Coley. He eventually gave a copy of his demo to Darryl Coley, who was the A&R Chief for Gospo Centric Records. This was a business venture launched by Vicki Mack-Lataillade, Darryl Coley, and his wife, Jenell Coley. Mrs. Mack-Lataillade had the production cleaned up and remixed to remove the flaws and eventually released the Family's self-titled CD debut. By July 1993 it had reached No. 32 on the gospel album sales charts. The single "The Reason Why We Sing" topped the gospel charts by December of 1993 and would gain a position one year later at the top of the R&B charts. The complete album went gold and reached number six on the R&B charts. In 1993, *Kirk Franklin and the Family* was the first gospel album to sell over one million copies (Carpenter, 2005).

Franklin had a sophomore CD project packaged and ready for release called *What Cha Lookin' 4*, yet the label decided to hold off on it and expedited a Christmas CD that was recorded in one day. *Jesus Is the Reason for the Season* became an R&B hit, developing a pattern for Franklin's hit-making formula (Carpenter, 2005).

In 1996, *What Cha Lookin' 4* outsold his debut album, presenting a more contemporary flavor as it topped the R&B charts at number three and number twenty-three on the *Billboard* 200. Franklin's hit-making formula demonstrated a pattern that would continue for his career. Never before in gospel had an artist repeatedly topped gospel and CCM charts, while gaining high positions on the R&B Charts and the *Billboard* 200. This success would soon be met by speculation of his authenticity for the message over the money and legal hardships (Turner, 2010).

Various sources have quoted Shirley Caesar, the first lady of gospel, in her comments concerning Franklin during this era. In an interview with *Gospel Music Today* magazine, she prophetically stated this:

> There were times when I would look at him and frown on it because I was not used to that type of gospel. But when the Clark Sister and the Hawkins Family came out, they called that contemporary. Twenty years later, it's traditional, compared to what we are listening to now. So give it another fifteen years and what he's doing will be traditional (Carpenter, 2005).

As a result of Franklin's rejuvenation of gospel music in the 1990s, other gospel artists benefited. He demonstrated an approach that gave gospel music a mass appeal, while not compromising the message, with a radical stance as a young believer. His dance moves and group choreography in the videos were an approach common to R&B and pop music, not gospel. Franklin "unleashed" gospel and brought the genre with him. Other labels began to increase the budgets for their gospel artists and invested more in marketing them. The trend he set continued with the 1996 hit "Melodies from Heaven" and God's Property hit "Stomp," which featured a Funkadelic undertone, sold two million copies, and spent two weeks at number one on the R&B singles chart (Carpenter, 2005).

Franklin's success was not celebrated by all. He was entangled with legal matters for royalties from members of the Family and God's Property. He was sued in 1998 by God's Property, based on the accusation that he had lured the group's founder into signing an "onerous and one-sided" contract. A few years later in 2000, Franklin and Gospo Centric Records were sued by the Family with a multi-million dollar lawsuit. They sought royalties from the Nu Nation Project. These legal matters swayed Franklin to become a solo artist (Carpenter, 2010).

Franklin's discography includes 12 albums: *Kirk Franklin and the Family* (1993), *Christmas* (1995), *Whatcha Lookin' 4* (1995), *God's Property* (1997), *Nu Nation Project* (1998), *Kirk Franklin Presents 1NC* (2000), *The Rebirth of Kirk Franklin* (2002, 2003), *9-Hero* (2005), *The Fight of My Life* (2007), *Hello Fear* (2011), *Losing My Religion* (2015) (All Music, 2015). His recognitions include nine Grammy Awards, one American Music Award, thirty-nine Stellar Awards (gospel), sixteen Dove Awards (CCM), eight NAACP Image Awards, two BET Music Awards, one Soul Train Award, and a host of other recognitions (Kirk Franklin, 2015).

Franklin married his long-time friend Tammy Collins in 1996. Together they have four children, including children from former relationships and two they had together. His strong family support and pastoral support from national public figure Pastor Tony Evans have helped him in his struggle to overcome an addiction to pornography and in growing in his call to public ministry. Unfortunately, his Aunt Gertrude passed away when he was 17 years old before she got a chance to see her investment in his talent and strict spiritual upbringing manifested (*Charisma* magazine website, 2015).

Despite these trials, Franklin has managed to have a body of work that includes CD albums, singles, DVD videos, over nine tours, work on the movie sound track of *Kingdom Come*, and the top-selling gospel album of all times, *The Preacher's Wife*. It featured Whitney Houston, who sang his composition "Joy" along with various songs by other artists (All Music, 2015). Franklin entered a joint venture in 2013 with RCA Records and established Fo Yo Soul Recordings. He is the host and executive producer of BET's *Sunday Best*, a gospel-singing competition that offers exposure to undiscovered gospel artists. As of May 2013, he can be heard on Kirk Franklin's *Praise* Sirius Radio channel 64 (Kirk Franklin, 2015).

Franklin is considered a top-selling producer in gospel music and has produced artists including Tamela Mann, Tasha Page-Lockhart, and The Walls Group (Collins, 2015). Other projects Franklin is involved with include the House of Blues Gospel Brunch experience, which features local artists singing material selected by him. He also can be seen hosting the *American Bible Challenge* game show, in which Bible enthusiasts share their knowledge of the Bible. Franklin's autobiography, *Church Boy: My Music & My Life*, released in 1998, covers his return to the industry after a nearly tragic ten-foot fall from the stage during his climb to fame. In his 2010 release, *The Blueprint: A Plan for Living above Life's Storms*, he shares insight and wisdom for building a fulfilled life (Kirk Franklin, 2015).

Dr. Teresa Hairston, publisher of one of the gospel music industry's leading trade magazines *Gospel Industry Today*, stated that Franklin bridged gospel music and secular listeners. She agrees with Franklin when he states that this is a success that could be authored only by God. His fusion of gospel with the mainstream audience was not something Franklin could manufacture. Hairston reveals to *Charisma* magazine that God did it, and He opened a door for Franklin to be used (*Charisma*, 2015). His compilation genius uniquely demonstrates an inspirational message that shows unity and diversity that overcome barriers of race, ethnicity, and genres, shattering barriers between the religious and secular communities. This is demonstrated in the hit song "Lean on Me," which features secular artists R. Kelly, Mary J. Blige, and Bono singing alongside sacred artist Crystal Lewis, the choir, and Kirk Franklin. A prior song, "Stomp," included rap artist Salt from the group Salt and Pepper. The dance-crazed video shocked the secular and sacred worlds as it depicted a visual for Franklin's hip-hop- oriented approach to gospel. Franklin bridged the gap between secular and sacred music with his collaborative projects and even with appearances in secular venues, such as the TV show *Soul Train* (Daniels, 2012).

Many gospel artists today are reaping the benefits of the struggles, rejections, and controversy Kirk Franklin endured. Artists are now able to operate with acceptance in venues that are gospel and R&B centric. Secular artists are now able to express their church roots and spirituality in gospel venues. The purposes and forms of gospel have expanded since Dorsey's inception that introduced the "sound" that has evolved for the past 85 years.

William Becton, artist-producer-pastor (an artist before his time). A contemporary of Kirk Franklin is an artist named William Earl Becton Jr. He is an extraordinarily multitalented artist whose musical style and innovation in some ways appeared to be before his time in the area of urban styles of gospel music. Becton is most known in the industry for his 1995 release "Be Encouraged" from the CD release *Broken*. His contributions, along with Franklin's, in the late 1990s helped to pave the way for more styles of crossover music that bridge sacred and secular listeners (All Music, 2015).

William Becton's musical journey began at the age of four in the church choir and continued at the age of eight, when he attended the Sewell Music Conservatory for voice in his native city, Washington, DC. He grew up in a middle-class Christian home with two parents and one sister where education and Christian values were instilled. Becton would eventually graduate from the famous Duke Ellington School of the Arts, a District of Columbia public high school dedicated to the arts in education. He would go on to study music education at the University of the District of Columbia. By this time he had already begun pursuing the music industry (williambecton.org). In 1991, Becton went from being an amateur aspiring artist to an industry professional when established gospel legends Timothy Wright and Myrna Summers recorded a song he wrote called "He's in the Midst of It All."

Becton would eventually break into the music industry as a national artist with overnight success with his debut self-produced album *Broken I* in 1995. Bill Carpenter, author of *Uncloudy Days: The Gospel Music Encyclopedia*, parallels the 1995 Oklahoma City terrorist bombing as the catalyst for the crossover success of the R&B-styled inspirational release "Be Encouraged." Washington, DC, station WPGC played their native son's release in memory of those who had died in the bombing. This led to a wave of black radio stations playing the release, a wave that eventually moved along the Atlantic coast stations, propelling it in a short time to a national hit. Shortly after this, Becton agreed to a distribution deal with Innersound Records, which positioned the *Broken* CD with national availability in stores. The CD spent 1 weeks as number one on the Billboard gospel charts and peaked at number 25 on the Billboard R&B Singles chart, selling over 300,000 copies (Carpenter, 2010).

At this time Becton was recording with his group, William Becton and Friends. Subsequent discography includes *Heart of a Love Song* (1997). It included a hip-hop single "Working Out," which reached number 54 on the R&B chart and number 5 on the gospel album chart. In 2000, he released *B2K: Prophetic Songs of Promise* and in 2003 *Broken Volume 2: Live.* His industry sustainability as an artist during this period was met with business challenges and label reorganizations. As a result, Becton began focusing his efforts on other ministry and industry activities. This included being a radio personality at WPGC and eventually on ABC radio's nationally syndicated show called *Rejoice* (Carpenter, 2010).

Becton focused on public ministry after being licensed in 1998 and ordained in 2002 in the AME Zion denomination. He became heavily involved in local church ministry. A vision for his own ministry began incubating from his own experiences as he birthed his ministry purpose, "making disciples of the broken." In 2005, William Becton relocated to Charlotte, North Carolina, where he pastored Kingdom Purpose Worship Center and continued his personal vision in ministry (williambecton.org).

Becton has not made major waves in the gospel music industry in over ten years. During this "pause" in his industry career, he has endured personal hardships, including the death of both parents, health challenges, financial woes, and divorce. Despite this, Becton has managed to "retreat, reload" and focus on "a relaunch" of ministry and industry focuses. He mentioned this in his 2010 Celebration of Achievement Event held in Charlotte. He has been focusing on a reinvention of himself, his ministry, and his industry pursuits in preparation for his next level (Becton's Celebration of Achievement sermon, 2010).

In the process, Becton has overcome health challenges and dropped over 150 pounds. He is in the process of compiling a documentary that speaks to his hiatus from the industry spotlight. He has preluded his return with the release of a free download *Thank You* (2012) and video that foreshadows the documentary. He has continued to stay connected with the industry and continues to be accessible for preaching engagements, music ministry, consulting/ teaching, and live concerts (williambecton.org).

His industry achievements include two Stellar Awards (including six Stellar Award nominations), two Gospel Music Workshop of America Excellence Awards, three Washington Area Music Awards, Dove Award nominations, and a Gold Record (williambecton.org). Becton's self-reinvention yielded the educational achievement of a bachelor of arts degree in 2010 and a master of theology degree in 2012, both from Life Christian Academy (Charlotte Campus). He is pursuing a PhD in theology at the same institution in the next few years (williambecton.org).

Now Pastor William Becton leads an urban-friendly ministry in Charlotte called House of Worship. This is done in parallel with a mobile ministry as a music minister extraordinaire and industry consultant in the church community. Additionally, his teachings and sermons impart spiritually to various aspects of church growth and provide practical relevance to life for Christians. His highly anticipated upcoming musical works will echo the message for personal spiritual growth and practical life situations (Becthoven Enterprises, 2015).

Becton's music ministry, gospel ministry, and gospel music industry acumen were all demonstrated in Raleigh, North Carolina, at the Gospel Music One Sound Music Seminar and Concert series held November 20–21, 2015 (Live Seminar, 2015). He stressed the importance of passion for ministry in all aspects, not just music. He stated that those who have a true passion for ministry do not get tired of doing it. These individuals will work on it day and night until they get sleepy, and they continue to do so even if they are not profiting financially. When people lose their passion for ministry, they need to step aside and let someone else take the position. A complete synopsis of his recommendations are included in Gospel Music One Sound results in chapter 6 and appendix 2 of this work (Live Performance, 2015).

He presented a live concert with William Becton and Friends at the Gospel Music One Sound Project Concert that demonstrated an urbanized approach to gospel music. The introduction song he arranged provided an opportunity for local group Blessed Union, The Group (featuring Reunion members), to work with an industry professional. Becton's approachability to the local church community and to aspiring gospel artists is a strength that will allow him to leverage a grass-roots connection for his relaunch to the mainstream gospel music industry (Live Performance, 2015).

The musical style demonstrated included an urban inspired arrangement of funk, R&B, and go-go instrumentation, coupled with inspiring, participatory, Christ-centered lyrics. The strong worship portion of the concert demonstrated the importance of technical ability so that spiritual anointing could set the atmosphere toward the scripture discussed in the seminar, 2 Chronicles 5:13–14. The evening closed out with everyone singing "Be Encouraged," with a remix vamp exemplary of Becton's innovation and musical sensitivity (Live Performance, 2015).

The unique appeal of BeBe and Cece Winans. The concept of sibling/family groups is common in music of all styles. Winans is a musical dynasty that is outstanding in Christian music, similarly to how the Jacksons and Osmonds reigned and impacted mainstream music. They have optimized this concept for three generations of music industry contributions that include parents Ma and Pop Winans, their ten children, and their grandchildren as singers, musicians, preachers, producers, and entrepreneurs in the music industry. The Detroit-based family began making waves in Christian music in the 1980s as brother-and-sister duo Benjamin "BeBe" Winans and Priscilla "CeCe" Winans Love, the seventh and eighth children of the Winans. Their trailblazing contributions include their cross-cultural appeal in mainstream, Christian contemporary and gospel music alike. BeBe and CeCe Winans were the first African-American artists to obtain significant airplay on Christian contemporary radio stations and the second African-American artists to receive a Dove Award in the "Group of the Year" category. Their entry into this predominantly white audience was launched by a five-year career on Jim Bakker's PTL Club televangelist ministry, begun in 1982. Their success as a duo group began with the release of "Up Where We Belong" for PTL Records, a remake of a popular mainstream song originally recorded by Joe Crocker. This was an idea of the first lady of the ministry, Tammy Bakker.

BeBe and CeCe Winans were like the Donnie and Marie Osmond of Christian music. Their entry into industry began with an inspirational approach and not the strong traditional churchy gospel sound that most African-American gospel artists were producing. Their time with the PTL Club uniquely positioned them as African-American artists. It gave them the space to pave the way for other gospel artists to cross over into the CCM, R&B, and pop genres.

As a sibling duo, BeBe and CeCe Winans produced nine albums from 1984 until 2009. They took a 15-year break from their duo work, pursued solo careers, and released "Still," which yielded two of their Grammy Awards. The albums and singles combined charted on the CCM, US Gospel, R&B, and pop charts. Most of their career as a duo occurred prior to the year 2000, but it paved the way for their very successful solo careers that launched in the new millennium and have continued to be sustainable until today. The duo received three Grammy Awards, nine Dove Awards, two NAACP Image Awards, two Soul Train Music Awards, numerous Stellar Awards, three Gold Albums, and one Platinum album.

Individually, BeBe Winans is recognized as a trailblazing gospel and R&B solo artist. He released seven solo albums from 1997 until 2012: *BeBe Winans* (1997), *Love and Freedom* (2000), *Live and Up Close* (2002*)*, *My Christmas Prayer* (2004), *Dream* (2005), *Cherch* (2007), and *America, America* (2012). His other contributions include establishing his own label, The Movement Group, in 2003; appearing as a judge on *Sunday Best*; and hosting a syndicated radio program called *The BeBe Winans Show*. He also had a star role as Harpo in the Broadway musical *Color Purple*, and he wrote a memoire about his close friend and musical icon Whitney Houston.

CeCe Winans has been considered the best-selling female gospel artist of all times, with over 12 million records sold worldwide. Her career includes the following album releases: *Alone in His Presence* (1995), *Everlasting Love* (1998), *His Gift* (1998), *Alabaster Box* (1999), *CeCe Winans* (2001), *Throne Room* (2003), *Purified* (2005), *Thy Kingdom Come* (2008), *Songs of Emotional Healing* (2010), and *For Always: The Best of CeCe Winans* (2010). Her industry awards include ten Grammy Awards, twenty Dove Awards, and seven Stellar Awards. CeCe Winans's other contributions include her own label, Pure Springs Gospel, and three books authored. She too was a close friend of Whitney Houston and sang the duet "Count on Me" with her on the movie soundtrack *Waiting to Exhale*.

CeCe and BeBe were honored in January 2016 as a duo at the Broadcast Music Inc. (BMI) Trailblazers of Gospel Music Awards in Atlanta. This is an elite invitation-only annual event in the industry. It was hosted by former recipient Yolanda Adams (Black Gospel website, 2015).

Contributions of Yolanda Adams. In *Uncloudy Days: The Gospel Music Encyclopedia*, Bill Carpenter (2005) refers to Yolanda Adams as the most heralded female gospel artist of the new millennium. She entered the gospel music industry in the 1990s with a traditional sound with signature tunes like "The Battle Is the Lord's" and "Through the Storm." Carpenter states that her 1999 *Mountain High, Valley Low,* album propelled her to superstardom (Carpenter, 2005). Adams is another gospel artist who is able to capture followers and audiences that bridge the gap between sacred and secular realms (Turner, 2010).

Yolanda Adams grew up in a middle-class family in Houston as the oldest of six children. Her musical influence came from her schoolteacher mom and high school coach dad, who were both great singers. In the Adams home she was exposed to a wide variety of music that included jazz, gospel, and classical. She admired James Cleveland, the Edwin Hawkins Singers, Nancy Wilson, and Stevie Wonder as her favorite singers. The family suffered the tragic death of her father, Major Adams, when Yolanda was 13 years old. He died from complications from injuries suffered in a car accident. Her mother, Carolyn, was devastated. Several years later, young Yolanda Adams chose to attend college at her father's alma mater, Texas Southern University. While living at home, she could still support her mom by helping raise her siblings (Carpenter, 2005).

Adams showed interest in a modeling career at one time and did an internship as a news anchor. These aspirations did not continue, so she chose to follow in the steps of her parents by becoming an elementary schoolteacher. Her weekends were spent singing in the Southeast Inspirational Choir, which is how she began making strides toward the gospel music industry. She was heard by Thomas Whitfield while singing with this choir. He worked with Yolanda in 1988 to record *Just As I Am*, an album originally composed for another singer. It landed a No. 8 position on the gospel charts, and her climb into the spotlight was on its way. She received support from legend Candi Staton and increased her exposure after appearing on Staton's TBN TV musical series called *New Direction* (Carpenter, 2005).

While Adam's career began to show promise, in her personal life she suffered a blow. She was married for two years and endured an abusive relationship. However, she did not let this distract her career focus. By now, Adams had left her teaching job and was a full-time gospel artist. Her business partners in the industry recognized that her beauty and talent gave her unique crossover appeal. After almost ten years in the industry, Adams moved to Elektra Records. This occurred after she was heard live and approached by the chairwoman Sylvia Rhone. They had a common vision for Adams that would allow her to remain gospel while dreaming big. She worked with Jimmy Jam and Terry Lewis, known for their transformation of R&B artists such as Janet Jackson. They released *Mountain High, Valley Low* in 1999. The album consisted of faith-inspired tracks with urban appeal. One of the songs, "That Name" by Richard Smallwood, was a bolder proclamation of faith. The album initially did not yield the charting performance anticipated. It was not until the third single, "Open My Heart," which Adams co-wrote, became popular that the project took root in the charts. It reached No. 10 on the Billboard R&B Single chart and No. 1 on the Radio and Records Urban AC chart. Eventually it was No. 1 on the gospel chart and CCM chart, No. 5 on the R&B album chart, and No. 24 on the pop album chart. *Mountain High Valley Low* sold double platinum units and delivered Adams her first Grammy Award for best contemporary soul gospel album in 2000 (Carpenter, 2005).

Yolanda Adams has continued to have sustainable success in the music and entertainment industry, not just in gospel music. Her complete discography includes these albums: *Just As I Am* (2008), *Through the Storm* (1991), *Save The World* (1993), *More Than A Melody* (1995), *Shakin' the House: Live in L.A.* (1996), *Yolanda, Live In Washington* (1996), *Battle Is the Lords* (1996), *Songs From the Heart* (1998), *Mountain High, Valley Low* (1999), *Christmas with Yolanda* (2000), *The Experience* (2001), *Believe* (2001), *Day by Day* (2005), *What a Wonderful Time* (2007), and *Becoming* (2011) (All Music, 2015). Yolanda Adams's music industry recognitions include four Grammy Awards, sixteen Stellar Gospel Music Awards, four Gospel Music Association's Dove Awards, one American Music Award, seven NAACP Image Awards, one Soul Train Music Award, and five BET Awards. In 2009, she was considered the number-one gospel artist of the last decade by *Billboard* magazine (All Music, 2015).

Today Yolanda Adams has mainstream presence in the industry in numerous facets. She has hosted the Stellar Awards and The Soul Train Awards and made numerous appearances on primetime and mainstream TV programs. She can be seen as a judge on BETs *Sunday Best*, hosted by Kirk Franklin, and can be heard on *The Yolanda Adams Morning Show* on 38 stations across the US (Yolanda Adams live website, 2015).

She has surpassed controversy about her presence in the secular markets. She is bold in her stance and belief that God told her she would be able to go into any genre of music or any platform to represent Him. As she began to bridge the gap between sacred and secular and to leverage the industry for ministry, there were grumblings from radio announcers that she was selling out for secular fame. They were uncomfortable with her hosting of the Soul Train Awards and with her being seen singing pop or doing tributes to secular artists. She stated that she is the same person regardless of the venue. She represents God everywhere. Carpenter (2005) references an interview Adams had with *Ebony* magazine where she speaks on the "too secular" controversy that has followed gospel artists before her. These trailblazers dared to be different, made adaptations, and evolved gospel music to the next formation. Adams states this:

> In Mahalia's day, folks told her the same thing. In Andraé Crouch's day, folks told him the same thing; in Thomas Dorsey's day, they told him the same thing. So I guess I'm on the right track.

Mary Mary: urban gospel duo. The trailblazing crossover success of Kirk Franklin, William Becton, and Yolanda Adams paved the way for Erica and Tina Campbell (formerly Atkins) as gospel and mainstream R&B artists. They have enjoyed over 20 years of sustainable success in the music industry after strategically placed milestones connected a path of ambition that continues today. They have endured beyond personal life challenges to sustain their industry status (Turner, 2010).

The duo grew up in a large family of nine children in Los Angeles, raised by a youth minister and choir director/evangelist in the Church of God in Christ. Their early beginnings included the group of siblings singing on *Bobby Jones Gospel* and 1995 casting in Michael Matthews's Chittlin' Circuit gospel plays. When not on the road, the sisters worked regular jobs to cover living expenses as they shared apartment rent. They both took background singing jobs with well-known R&B artists. Erica sang background for Brian McKnight and Brandy while Tina sang for Eric Benet and Kenny Lattimore. Meanwhile, they wrote gospel-oriented songs when they were not on the road. In 1996, the duo met producer Warren Campbell, connected with his church background, and began making history. They wrote collaboratively, eventually landing a publishing agreement with his publisher EMI Music. Their first industry entry was through the soundtracks for *Dr. Doolittle* and *The Prince of Egypt*. The duo signed with Columbia Records in 1999, continuing ongoing relationships with gospel artists. These relationships started with queen of gospel Mahalia Jackson, then passed to modern contemporary gospel artist Tremaine Hawkins, and then to urban contemporary singers Erica and Tina Campbell. The name Mary Mary, suggested by Warren Campbell, represents Mary Magdalene and Jesus's mother, who evangelized the love of Jesus as they supported His ministry (Carpenter, 2010).

Mary Mary established themselves in the industry with the successful launch of their urban single "Shackles," which was on their debut CD *Thankful*. This single charted at No. 9 on the R&B chart, No. 28 on the Hot 100, and as a Top Ten pop hit in England, France, the Netherlands, and Australia. As a result, they received a Grammy award for "Best Contemporary Gospel Album," two Dove Awards, three Stellar Awards, and a Soul Train Award (Carpenter, 2010). Today they have four Grammy Awards, two American Music Awards, eighteen Stellar Awards, four NAACP Image Awards, a Soul Train Award, and two BET Awards. This was done in parallel to yielding an exhaustive list of *Billboard* single and album chart successes that have continued since their entry to the industry (All Music, 2015).

The discography ensued since their entry to the music industry includes these albums: *Thankful* (2000), *Incredible* (2002), *Mary Mary* (2005), *A Mary Mary Christmas* (2006), *The Sound* (2008), *Something Big* (2011), and *Go Get It* (2012). Their crossover appeal that helps bridge sacred and secular audiences is driven by their mission to send uplifting messages through music and words that are relatable to everyone (I Love Mary Mary website, 2013).

The Marys, as they are often called, are part of a family music and entertainment dynasty. They have overlapping music efforts that work in parallel with Erica Atkins Campbell's husband, Warryn Cambell, a well-established music industry producer in his own right. His artists include Kanye West and Alicia Keyes. Tina Atkin Campbell's husband, Teddy Campbell, is an industry professional drummer for Ricky Minor's band and was seen on *Jay Leno's The Tonight Show*. In their spare time, Warryn and Teddy are part of a gospel quartet group The Soul Seekers, which was established in 2000. Teddy is the lead singer, and they have their own series of accolades and hits (I Love Mary Mary website, 2013).

Erica and Tina each have recently enjoyed individuality with their own solo careers, which have benefited from the foundation laid by their success with Mary Mary. Their brands as solo artists also benefited from the *Mary Mary* series on WE TV that launched in 2012. The reality TV show completed four seasons as of 2015, and the stars opened their personal lives to the world. In addition to their business challenges and industry decisions, the primetime TV audience saw Erica and Tina operate busy households, raise children, coordinate support with their sisters and mother, endure the death of their father, Eddie Atkins, and experience the recovery of Tina and Teddy's marriage from Teddy's confession of infidelity. During this, solo career interest ensued and unfolded. They have joined the ranks of other gospel artists with reality TV shows. They are the subject of controversy from the Black Church as to whether this form of entertainment is more money driven than message driven. Other regular media presence includes being judges on Kirk Franklin's brainchild *Sunday Best* TV show and guest radio personalities for Thanksgiving 2015 on his Channel 64 Sirius *Praise* (I Love Mary Mary website, 2013).

Warryn and Erica Campbell recently launched a church, following Warryn's call to the ministry. He was licensed to preach in 2009 by Bishop Kenneth Ulmer at Faithful Central Bible Church in Inglewood, California, and was ordained February 1, 2015, by Bishop Ulmer to fulfill his 2014 call to plant the church. Pastor Warryn and First Lady Erica launched California Worship Center in North Hollywood as a place that provides inspiration and love to its worshipers (California Worship Center website, 2015).

The future holds great promise for this duo as they continue to demonstrate that gospel artists can be diversified in the entertainment industry and deliver sustainable results. From a ministry perspective, they continue to bridge the sacred and secular worlds while keeping their message of Christ as the focus of all they do. Mary Mary was honored in January 2016 as a duo at the Broadcast Music Inc. (BMI) Trailblazers of Gospel Music Awards in Atlanta. This is based primarily on their strides in gospel music in the new millennium.

Israel Houghton connects praise and worship to the Black Church. As mentioned in gospel music historian Bob Marovich's interview, the new millennium brought with it a connection to the genre of praise and worship in the Black Church. The lyrics were simple and easy for congregations to sing by call and response. This genre, which was launched in the white evangelical and CCM audience, was an adaptation of the devotional style singing led by

Pentecostal, Holiness, and Church of God in Christ denominations. Chord structure, musical arrangement, and instrumentation were not the "sound" the Black Church was used to hearing, yet this new commercialized approach slowly began to take root. Black Church musicians and choir directors began to improvise this genre in the same way hymns had been "gospelized" in the pre-gospel and traditional gospel eras (Marovich, 2015).

One artist who rose to prominence and helped set trends of gospel music with praise and worship was Israel Houghton. His talents include those as worship leader, songwriter, singer, producer, and accomplished musician. His music appeals cross-culturally and cross-denominationally to CCM and contemporary gospel audiences alike. His lyrics are primarily praise and worship focused, and the musical instrumentation fuses gospel, jazz, rock, and reggae. Houghton is biracial, and his music appeals to a diverse audience. Houghton worked full time in worship ministry in 1989 (Carpenter, 2005).

Similar to Kirk Franklin, in Houghton's early life the odds for success were against him. He was born to a 17-year-old unwed white teenage mother and an African-American father. They were not ready for parenting. They lived at the time in Waterloo, Iowa. When his mom's parents learned that their daughter was pregnant by an African-American, they wanted her to leave or abort the unborn child. She decided to keep Israel and moved to San Diego. One day as she was walking down the street aimlessly, a woman approached her, witnessed to her about Christ, and gave her a Bible. While she read through it, the name Israel was seen on pages she turned to. This is how she decided to name her son Israel (All Music, 2015).

Houghton grew up in the church environment, eventually becoming a full-time worship leader in 1989 at Lakewood Church, where internationally renowned Joel Osteen is the senior pastor of the megachurch. He landed an opportunity to tour with Fred Hammond and Radical for Christ. His first CD, *Whisper It Loud*, was released in 1995 with the group Houghton and his wife Meleasa had founded called New Breed Ministries. It was not until the new millennium that his 2002 CD, *Real*, and the 2004 CD, *Live from Another Level*, launched him in the industry. The singles "There's a Lifting of Hands" and "Again I Say, Rejoice" propelled Israel and New Breed to the next level (Carpenter, 2005).

Houghton's discography includes the following albums: *New Season* (2001), *Real* (2002), *Live from Another Level* (2004), *A Deeper Level: Live* (2007), *Israel and New Breed Smooth Jazz Tribute* (2007), *The Power of One* (2009), *Love God, Love People: The London Sessions* (2010), *Decade* (2012), *Jesus at the Center: Live* (2012), and *Covered: Alive in Asia* (2015). Houghton has additional recordings, such as collaborations and singles (All Music, 2015). His awards include five Grammy Awards, thirteen Dove Awards, two Stellar Awards, and a Soul Train Music Award (All Music, 2015).

He has uniquely been able to connect to the Black Church in a way that only his persona can execute. Houghton focuses on praise and worship and has delivered it on highly acclaimed platforms such as the Promise Keepers, Champions for Christ, Hillsong Conference 2006–2010 and Hillsong Conference Europe 2008–2010. His accessibility and approachability allow him to make an impact on the local church. At Donnie McClurkin's Perfecting Music Conference, Houghton taught the praise and worship course (All Music, 2015). He noted that effective worship has everything to do with one's heart.

> We must understand what it is and what it is not. It has very little to do with music. Everyone can worship, even if they are tone deaf. Worship is not just singing. Singing is a part of one's worship life. Sunday is usually the only time we see worship happening. The way we conduct our lives and the way we interact with people is an act of worship. Heart placement is vital to effective worship.

In corporate praise and worship, in church, effective worship is centered on whatever the goal is for those gathering.

Houghton went on to speak about how he has seen people get healed in worship services. He has experienced noted documented miracles during worship. The atmosphere of expectation is the breeding ground for the miraculous (I. Houghton, personal communication, April 30, 2011).

Houghton's contributions to gospel music in the new millennium is a part of the trend of artists whose music and approach unleash barriers. For Houghton, the unleashed barriers are racial divides, denominational barriers, cultural musical preferences, and generational gaps. He continues the evolution of gospel music with these necessary adaptations for praise and worship that promote unification within the church.

Lecrae: transcending mainstream as a hip-hop artist of Christian faith. The rise of hip-hop in the gospel genre is another demonstration of limitations unleashed and sacred-meeting-secular, all influenced by the young generation. In the new millennium, Christian hip-hop proved itself as a sustainable sub-genre that surpassed and dominated sales and chart position in gospel music. One artist who has been the trailblazer leading this movement with success in business and ministry is DeVaughn Lecrae Moore. His charting positions in September 2015 made *Billboard* history (All Music, 2015).

Lecrae Moore, born October 9, 1979, grew up living at risk and on a path of destruction. He was born to a single mother in Houston and a drug-using father he never met. In his early life, he lived in San Diego, Denver, and Dallas. His troubled childhood included molestation, abuse, and neglect. As a teenager, Lecrae was into using drugs, stealing, and fighting and was headed toward gang life. Rap music became his outlet to express himself, and the lifestyle of rappers in secular hip-hop culture was attractive to him. He looked up to these images and began to emulate negative traits. While living this fast-paced life of destruction, he was influenced by a spiritual grandmother, who constantly tugged at his soul to live for Christ. While he was a drug dealer, he clutched onto the Bible she gave him as a way of protection. As a result, when he got arrested for drug possession, the officer saw the Bible and let him go only if he promised to start living by it. However, Moore still lived the life of a thrill seeker, trying to fill his voids with worldly means. At the age of 17 he began attending church after many years of ignoring his grandmother's wishes (All Music, 2015).

Moore's conversion began at age 19 when he saw the Christian hip-hop group the Cross Movement. He was able to relate to them culturally and to their love and conviction for Christ. When God spared his life from a terrible car crash, completely uninjured, he returned to college for a fresh start. He became a "street evangelist," sharing his printed testimony. As he continued to mature spiritually, he committed to spending his life spreading hope and encouragement through his music and volunteerism (All Music, 2015).

Moore co-founded Reach Records when he was 25 years old and released *Real Talk*, later released by Cross Movement Records. This release charted for 12 weeks at No. 29 on the *Billboard* gospel albums. It was also during this time that he co-founded the non-profit organization called RealLife Ministries. It is a training institute for Christian leaders on biblical teachings and how to make the Word relevant to hip-hop culture (All Music, 2015).

From this moment forward, he would sustain a successful career as a hip-hop artist in the industry. His full discography includes *Real Talk* (2005), *After the Music Stops* (2006), *Rebel* (2008), *Rehab* (2010), *The Overdose* (2011), *Gravity* (2012), and *Anomaly* (2014). Moore's *Anomaly* made *Billboard* history as the first album to be the No. 1

album on both the gospel albums and *Billboard* Top 200 lists. It is also recognized as the fifth album ever to be on both the Christian albums chart and the *Billboard* 200 simultaneously (All Music, 2015).

Moore also has filmography of seven releases, and he has received three Stellar Awards, two Grammy Awards, five Dove Awards, and one *Billboard* Music Award. In the music industry, Moore's music transcends genres, allowing his message for Christ to have a broader platform (All Music, 2015).

He made waves in the mainstream arena in 2012 and 2013 with the release of *Gravity* and *Church Clothes* and has continued to sustain mainstream relevance. This is evident with his routine presence on mainstream talk shows such as *The Tonight Show*, starring Johnny Fallon, and the media coverage he obtains in mainstream publications. Media include *Rolling Stone, Vibe, New York Times, The Huffington Post,* and the industry recognized trade publication *Billboard* magazine. His mainstream relevance is most evident in his inclusion with mainstream hip-hop artists in events such as The 2013 Rock the Bells Tour with hip-hop legends such as Wu-Tank Clan, Rakim, and Common. Moore was the coheadliner in the tour Winter Jam, which sold 557,000 tickets. It is recognized as the number-one selling tour in the country, outselling Beyonce, Disney, Justin Timberlake, and Elton John (Lacrae website, 2015).

In addition to RealLife Ministries, Moore uses his industry platform for ministry in other ways beyond music. He is a spiritual advisor to professional athletes and offers free-of-charge chapel services before professional sports games. He also participated with other celebrities in *This Is Fatherhood*, a part of President Obama's administration's Fatherhood and Mentoring Initiative. This effort was devoted to restoring America's commitment to healthy fatherhood (Lacrae website, 2015).

Today Moore resides in Atlanta with his wife, Darragh Moore, whom he met before his conversion. They have three children they are raising as a Christian family. His approach to leveraging fame and fortune for The Father gospel choir is a perfect example of how an independent artist can balance ministry in the industry. Despite the spotlight, he remains humble and gives all credit to his savior, Jesus Christ (Lecrae website, 2015).

CHAPTER 4

Research Methodology: Explication of the Analytical Approach

The research was designed for an analysis inclusive of trends identified in the emerging gospel music industry past and present and to provide practical tools and applications for improved effectiveness of gospel music practitioners today. This purpose was deemed best to address the problem statement by investigation of the hypothesis: The problem is that the independent gospel artist is challenged to balance ministry against the demands of the music industry. As a disciple of Christ, the independent gospel artist is expected to spread the gospel through song while not compromising or conforming to the conflicting values of the music industry aimed at mainstream cultural appeal. In other words, how does the independent gospel artist balance ministry focus against the demands of the industry and sustain effectiveness without compromising his or her Christian faith?

As a hypothesis, the history of gospel music demonstrates continuity in the elements of gospel music with necessary adaptations, in an accepted form, from the Dorsey to the Franklin eras. As gospel music has evolved, so has the social acceptance of what was once controversial in art form, practices, and venue. This has liberated the next generation of gospel artists to have greater opportunity for ministry while leveraging the music industry.

Research Design

The findings were obtained from a combined bibliographic and descriptive research design. From a bibliographic perspective, this included a theological look at African-American worship and spirituality and a scholastic literature review to trace the evolution of gospel music. From a descriptive perspective, this included field research obtained from human experience. It was ethnographic in nature and was obtained from observations, interviews, conferences, survey collections, online discussions, and secondary data analysis.

Research Method

A mixed method approach of qualitative and quantitative research was identified as the most appropriate research method for this project. The mixed method was appropriate for several reasons. 1) Just as Dr. Raymond Wise (2002) pointed out, there is a lack of one comprehensive source that houses the historical development of gospel music, a key component of the African-American worship experience and a systematic literature review. 2) No single method was found to be the best fit to address the problem statement and also to investigate the hypothesis. A qualitative approach fit the problem while a quantitative and qualitative approach investigated the hypothesis. 3)

The assumption to claiming knowledge on the topic was real world and practical oriented with attention focused more on the research problem than a commitment to one philosophy in how to obtain the research. For these three reasons, flexibility in research methods is necessary to be able to use what is best for the circumstance at hand.

Additionally, I have drawn from my professional experience as an engineer in my research approach. I hold a bachelor of science degree in mechanical engineering, and I have approximately 20 years of experience in problem solving in manufacturing and service-oriented applications. For the past eight years I have worked leading projects and applying problem-solving tools for business improvement using a problem-solving methodology called Six Sigma. I am internationally certified through the American Society of Quality and work as a Six Sigma Master Black Belt for a Fortune 500 manufacturer. I teach Six Sigma training for the corporate office and coach others on how to apply it in their daily work.

As defined by the *isixsigma* website (2015), Six Sigma is a disciplined, data-driven approach and methodology for eliminating defects (driving toward six standard deviations between the mean and the nearest specification limit) in any process—from manufacturing to transactional and from product to service. The aim is to improve the customer's experience. These can be internal and external customers. In the science of quality, Six Sigma has had deep roots in the business decisions, growth, and sustainability of companies such as Motorola in the 1980s, General Electric in the 1990s, and many others that followed.

This methodology is no longer used in just manufacturing environments; it is now also widely used in environments for services or non-statistical applications. This is a highly sought-after skill set in areas such as the medical field, life insurance, finance, call centers, order processing, school systems, and the government. It removes waste in organizational processes in order to improve productivity, optimize spending, enhance efficiency, and minimize defects. I naturally apply Six Sigma concepts and tools in practical life experiences and have applied these tools and concepts in my ministry pursuits. At present there are limited examples to demonstrate Six Sigma being used in ministry, but as people receive the training in other industries and fields of work, they will discover opportunities to apply it in ministry.

The DMAIC methodology from the Six Sigma tool set fits nicely in this research approach to improve the existing process of an independent gospel artist to effectively execute ministry in the industry. DMAIC is an acronym for Define, Measure, Analyze, Improve, and Control. These are the phases used for improving an existing process. Specific tools apply to each phase. We will apply it several times in the overall approach and as a method for arriving at improvements in practical ministry use.

Another tool from the Six Sigma tool set we will apply is the SWOT Analysis. This is an acronym for Strengths, Weakness, Opportunities, and Threats. This tool is used for strategic planning in business, yet it can also be used for short-term and practical applications in other organizational situations. During this project and in my music ministry consulting work, I have used this tool as a quick approach to collect and organize qualitative data and arrive at solutions for strategy and vision planning in music ministry.

Explication of the Analytical Approach

Define the problem is the first step in the analytical approach used. This parallels with the first phase of the Six Sigma DMAIC approach. It also includes gaining an understanding of the background and current situation. The problem was defined in the problem statement. From a qualitative standpoint, ethnographic means were used to begin researching the problem through my participation in various field experiences. I compiled response papers that documented observations and interview notes and compiled videos. These were from attending the 2011 Perfecting Music Conference sponsored by Donnie McClurkin, the 2012 Gospel Music Workshop of America session, and 2012–2014 Stellar Awards week events. I attended these sessions for my professional development as a gospel music artist and a church music ministry professional. I sought to apply and teach what I learned to members of my ensemble—Blessed Union, The Group—and music ministry work at Oak City Baptist Church in Raleigh.

My personal knowledge of leveling and gaining an understanding of the background of African-American worship developed through field experience. This included attending the *African-American Church Music Series* with Dr. James Abbington in 2011, the Homiletics, Hymns and Spirituals Conference featuring Dr. James Abbington and Dr. Luke Powery in 2011, and "African-American Music and Worship," taught by Dr. Raymond Wise at the Gospel Music Workshop of America 2012. A systematic literature view occurred in readings required for the course in African-American spirituality with Dr. Anthony Hunt (2014) and recommended readings from scholars I found through research and consultation. This included extensive consultation by Prof. L. Stanley Davis (2014) and two webinars he conducted on Chicago's Roots in Gospel Music (2015). These will be discussed further in the research intervention.

Measure is the second phase of the DMAIC approach. Measuring the current situation by data collection provides a baseline to be used for analysis. Data collection for the problem statement and the hypothesis under investigation occurred through several paths. These paths can be categorized as field experience, organization of trends identified in the literature review, and an effort I organized called the Gospel Music One Sound Project. Field experience from conferences mentioned earlier was qualitative and ethnographic in nature. Additional ethnographic resources used include media, trade magazines, and websites, along with articles and publications (hardcopy and electronic), and information directed by the consultation of subject matter experts, journalists, and scholars in the field. I organized into tables a collection of identified influences and trends in the review of historical literature. This prepared the qualitative attributes compiled for a non-empirical assessment.

The Gospel Music One Sound Project occurred November 1–23, 2015. This was an effort I organized using Facebook as an online platform for dialogue on the problem statement as a tool for investigating the hypothesis and as a marketing tool to promote onsite music seminars and concerts. These activities were used as a part of the intervention. Invitations were sent to my network of Facebook friends and other Facebook groups aimed at gospel music and gospel artists. The research population consisted of African-Americans who are practitioners of gospel music in the African-American worship experience. The online group consisted of approximately 80 members across the United States, 30 of whom actively participated as a focus group in two survey instruments primarily located in and near Raleigh. I designed the surveys using a software called Survey Monkey. The first survey instrument used qualitative and quantitative methods aimed at investigating the hypothesis as a pre-test and post-test on awareness provided during the three-week time frame. The second survey instrument called Music Ministry Development used a qualitative approach aimed at identifying issues in the local church music ministry. Profile information on church roles and responsibilities, years of experience, and denominations were anonymously collected. These are described in further detail in chapter 5 (Presentation and Analysis) in the "Field Experience" section. A Likert scale and quantitative method was used to quantify the results of the questions on trends in attitude. Attribute and descriptive data were collected from demographics compiled on gender, race, age, denomination, roles, responsibilities, educational background, and employment status of the research population.

Such data are useful for collecting culturally specific research that provides information on values, opinions, behaviors, and social contexts of a particular population.

Analyze is the third phase of the DMAIC approach, and it aligns with standard doctoral research. Survey Monkey was used to compile graphical representations of data trends on the survey instruments. The SWOT analysis was used as an exercise with day-one seminar participants to analyze their personal ministry and industry pursuits. These will be presented in the presentation and analysis chapter, along with trends identified from manual data collection and analysis from the systematic literature review.

Improve and **Control** are the final phases of the DMAIC approach. They will be discussed in subsequent chapters along with findings and prescriptions. African-American worship experience is dynamic and continuously evolving due to daily impacts from African-American culture. This approach arrives at best practices and trends of influential artists, industry professionals, and local church/community music ministry leaders in current times. When these elements are coupled with supportive changes in social acceptance, attitude, or perception, the environment for transformation and possibilities is fertilized. Thus, sustainable and effective improvements can take root.

In concluding this chapter, it is important to note the challenge of researching a specialized topic that is alive, dynamic, and still evolving. The African-American worship experience, in terms of ministry and the industry of gospel music, is influenced by an emerging African-American culture. Thus, maintaining relevance requires continuous monitoring and reporting. Having a research method that will sustain relevance and that can be replicated over time will be useful for continuous study.

CHAPTER 5

Presentation and Analysis

The content in this chapter is based on data and information gathered from an assessment of the literature and an analysis of the field experience. The assessment reveals how the problem of balancing ministry against industry has been ongoing and existing since the early evolution of the industry. It also supports the hypothesis on how social acceptance follows what was initially rejected. As mentioned in the prior chapter, it was deemed best for this study to address the problem statement by investigation of the hypothesis. For convenience, the problem statement and hypothesis are presented below for reference:

> The problem is that the independent gospel artist is challenged to balance ministry against the demands of the music industry. As a disciple of Christ, the independent gospel artist is expected to spread the gospel through song, while not compromising and conforming to the conflicting values of the music industry aimed at mainstream cultural appeal. In other words, how does the independent gospel artist balance ministry focus against the demands of the industry and sustain effectiveness without compromising his or her Christian faith?

> As a hypothesis, the history of gospel music demonstrates continuity in the elements of gospel music with necessary adaptations in an accepted form from the Dorsey to the Franklin era. As gospel music has evolved, so has the social acceptance of what was once controversial in art form, practices, and venue. This has liberated the next generation of gospel artists to have greater opportunity for ministry while leveraging the music industry.

Assessment of the Literature

Prior to the birth of the gospel music genre in approximately 1930, black sacred music in various forms was generally heard only in church. See Image 8 in Appendix 1 for the historical time frames discussed prior to the era of traditional gospel music.

Pre-Gospel Era, Pre-1900, (Pre- and Post-Emancipation)
Ditties, Hollers, and Spirituals

During this era, gospel music had not yet been conceptualized, and there was not a sacred music venue outside the church. Therefore, the problem statement does not apply. There was no gospel music industry, and the only venue for black sacred music was the church, as illustrated in Figure 1 at the end of this section. In summary of the first pre-gospel era prior to 1900, the hypothesis is demonstrated in various aspects, even before gospel music has been developed. Since gospel music is not yet formed, the term *black sacred music* is used in this section in order to include the elements that are predecessors of gospel music.

Folk spirituals start the continuum of black sacred music before gospel music evolves. This was the style sung by slaves on the plantation. This occurs before the Dorsey era, yet it stills holds true. Spirituals were an early expression of the souls of black folks. See Figure 1 at the end of this section for a visual aid of this continuum for this era.

Folk spirituals and work songs alike were controversial in the eyes of the slaveholder. An accepted adaptation occurred when they were "Europeanized" and later appreciated by whites and elite blacks as a result of the new style harmonies demonstrated by the Fisk Jubilee Singers. A compilation of this is available in Table 1-A at the end of this section.

The Fisk Jubilee Singers were early trailblazers as gospel artists and influenced the gospel music industry. Not only did they contribute stylistic practices to the art form, but they also planted the concept of crossover appeal and of "paid" performance outside of worship services. Their international travels and performances before kings and queens were significant in demonstrating early possibilities of the marketability of black sacred music. They leveraged industry to expand ministry when they "commercialized" the material for European appeal in exchange for funding for Fisk University. Their mission was ministry focused as they served the African-American community with their talents, singing songs with lyrics that preserved the demonstration of God in African-American history. This concept was also ministry of justice in the mental breakthrough realized by whites from dignified black performers. Prior to the Fisk Jubilee Singers, most black performers or entertainers had to be minstrel shows or jokesters that did not depict black culture as a serious art form. They created a worship space outside the four walls of the church and established an international venue that generated $150,000 over seven years (Fisk Jubilee Singers, 2015). This set the template and stage for other historically black college and university (HBCU) jubilee singers to follow for generations. As the hypothesis states, they "liberated" HBCU students of other schools to leverage the commercialization of Negro spirituals for ministry in similar regards. Refer to Table 1-B for a visual of this summary.

Figure 1: Continuum of Black Sacred Music (Pre-Gospel Era)

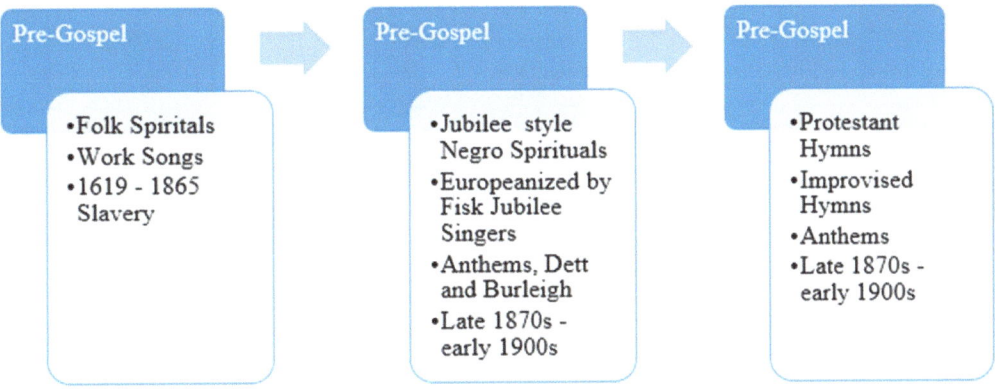

The Pre-Gospel Era (1619–1865 to Early 1900s)
Black Sacred Music Social Acceptance vs. Evolution of Black Sacred Music

Table 1-A

What was controversial or rejected? When did it occur?	Practitioner	Who rejected it?	Who accepted it?	When was it accepted?	What contributions evolved black sacred music/gospel music?
Drumbeats played and folk spirituals, work songs. During slavery 1619–1865. Post-Emancipation 1866–1871.	Slaves.	Some slaveholders rejected it for fear that the music encoded messages.	Some slaveholders accepted it as amusement. Slaves who created and sang it accepted it.	Spirituals were more widely accepted by whites after the Fisk Jubilee Singers reinvented them with Westernized harmonies as concert anthems.	Art form: Field ditties and work songs were the predecessors of blues, ragtime, and jazz, later fused in gospel music. Spirituals were the predecessors of gospel music. Provided a pathway for classically trained black composers of black sacred music.
Improvised hymns. Post-Emancipation 1880s–early 1900s.	Black congregants.	White affiliate churches/ some elite blacks.	Sanctified black churches.	Later accepted in developmental years of gospel 1920s–1930s.	Predecessor to gospel music.

The Pre-Gospel Era (Prior to 1900)
Influences on the Evolution of the Gospel Music Industry
A Compilation of Contributions in Art Form, Practices (Industry/Ministry), and Venues

Table 1-B

Contributor	Art Form	Practices	Venues
Fisk Jubilee Singers 1871.	Concert-style Negro spirituals (jubilee singing).	*Industry:* Stylistic practice. Westernized harmony/arrangements fused with African-American cultural expressions. Marketing practice demonstrated crossover appeal. Paid performing: the first documented for black sacred music. *Ministry:* Served the community with their talent by using it to raise funds for the operation of Fisk University. This was a trend for other HBCUs to follow. Broke racial barriers as they portrayed a dignified display of black talent. It demanded a respect of blacks in the arts/entertainment not yet earned by whites. Paved the way for black composers.	Concert halls. International acclaim beyond the church. The Fisk Jubilee Singers had a touchpoint with the industry with their recording of "There Is a Balm in Gilead" in 1909.

Pre-Gospel Era (1900–1920), Empowerment by Education
Negro Spirituals/Anthems

In summary of this era, the influence and empowerment of education were evident in black sacred music and its evolution toward the platform of the current-day gospel artist. As mentioned in the prior section, since gospel music was not yet formed, the term *black sacred music* is used to include the elements that were predecessors of gospel music. Again, there is not yet a gospel music industry for which the problem statement can be applied.

As reviewed prior on Figure 1, the continuum of black sacred music, continuity was now demonstrated in Negro spirituals with yet another adaptation in an accepted form. Burleigh and Dett composed and published arrangements of Negro spirituals with the influence of their classical music training.

During this era, evolving social acceptance was evident in the new interest of whites in black sacred music, as already shown on Table 1-A, mentioned in the prior section. White publishing companies invested in publishing sheet music of black composers. Burleigh and Dett, now the next generation, benefited from the labor of the Fisk Jubilee Singers when they were accepted for classical training at white universities, when they were allowed to perform at predominantly white international venues and prestigious concert halls, and when they removed racial barriers of opportunities traditionally off limits to blacks. Burleigh and Dett pioneered participation for blacks in ASCAP and in other community and industry activities. They leveraged their industry benefits as community servants by paving the way for others to follow and by creating opportunities. Dett left a legacy that would impact African-American worship for years to come when he founded the Hampton Institute Choral Union and the Hampton School of Music. These entities continue to be impactful components today in the growth of music ministry at the local church, in the community, in academia, and in the gospel music industry. Refer to Table 1-C for a visual aid of these elements.

The Pre-Gospel Era (1900–1920)
Influences on the Evolution of the Gospel Music Industry
A Compilation of Contributions in Art Form, Practices (Industry/Ministry), and Venues

Table 1-C

Contributor	Art Form	Practices	Venues
Harry Burleigh (Classically Trained Composer).	Classically influenced arrangements of Negro spirituals.	*Industry:* Burleigh published arrangements of spirituals for a solo voice and piano.	Concert halls. International acclaim beyond the church.
	Dett set folk songs and spirituals to choral and piano compositions in a romantic style.	Burleigh was a founding member of the American Society of Composers, Authors, and Publishers (ASCAP), and Dett was an early black member.	The Black Church. White churches. Synagogues (Burleigh).
Nathaniel Dett (Classically Trained Composer).	Dett introduced anthems to the Black Church.	White publishers invested in black sacred music, creating black opportunities. *Academia:* Dett founded the Hampton Institute Choral Union and the Hampton School of Music. *Ministry:* Strides in social justice gained as Burleigh broke race barriers when he sang and worked at churches and synagogues that traditionally did not allow black worshipers.	Community/Academia (Dett taught 20 years at Hampton Institute).

Development (1920s–1930s) and Traditional Gospel Era (1930–1945)
The Harlem Renaissance/ New Negro Movement
Gospel Hymnody/Gospel Genre

In summary of this era, gospel music was not initially accepted in every black church due to its resemblance in musical sound to secular blues, the other "soul" music. Over time it became an ecumenically accepted form in black churches, thanks to the pioneering by Thomas A. Dorsey, Dr. C. A. Tindley, Lucie Campbell, Sallie Martin, Roberta Martin, and many others who helped promote it.

On Figure 2 at the end of this section, the continuum of gospel music from arranged Negro spirituals to gospel hymnody to gospel songs is demonstrated. Tindley, the godfather of gospel music, began writing call-and-response, congregational-style hymns, with piano and organ. These were similar to spirituals, with the adaptation of instrumentation and the verse-chorus structure. Like Dorsey's songs, they were best demonstrated by performance instead of notation. Lucie Campbell's early music and publication of *Gospel Pearls* reflected gospel hymn style.

The problem statement cannot be applied to this era until post-1930. Yet the hypothesis is demonstrated in the developmental ages of gospel music as outlined in Table 2-A. Their style of music was initially more accepted in the Pentecostal churches and did not gain acceptance in Protestant churches until Campbell's influence of the National Baptist Convention provided the platform for exposure. Both composers paved the way for Dorsey and the contributions he and his peers of early gospel music would add. Dorsey evolved the gospel hymnody with the adaptation of blues progressions. Table 2-B at the end of this section shows evidence of the existing problems that brought about the industry for the early gospel-artists–in-the-making. The lack of acceptance supports the hypothesis, and eventual acceptance occurs in the golden age era.

Figure 2 Continuum of Gospel Music (Developmental and Traditional Gospel Era)

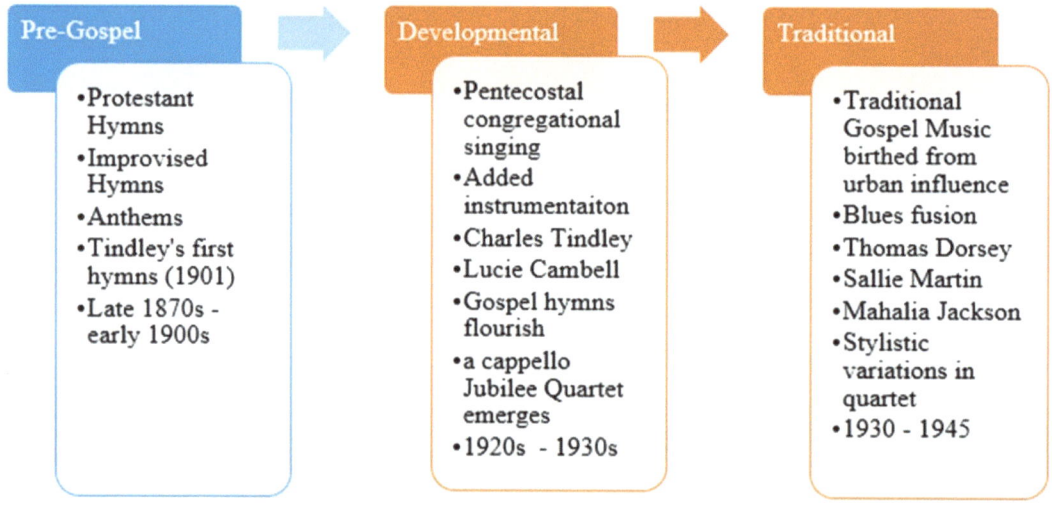

Development (1920s-1930s) and Traditional Gospel Era (1930-1945)
The Harlem Renaissance/New Negro Movement/Gospel Hymnody/Gospel Genre
Gospel Music Social Acceptance vs. Evolution of Gospel Music

Table 2-A

What was controversial or rejected? When did it occur?	Practitioner	Who rejected it?	Who accepted it?	When was it accepted?	What contributions evolved black sacred music/gospel music?
Gospel hymnody; traditional gospel music (fusion of blues with hymns) (1930s).	C. Tindley L. Campbell T. Dorsey S. Martin R. Martin (as examples)	The mainline black churches.	C.O.G.I.C Pentecostal Holiness Sanctified churches. Non-church venues.	During the golden age of gospel starting in the early 1940s.	Lucie Campbell's influence in the Baptist National Convention USA, Inc. Publication of *Gospel Pearls*. Additional instrumentation and stylistic changes made a distinct art form. NCGCC, 1932. Rejection yielded a gospel circuit venue and launched an industry.

What was controversial or rejected? When did it occur?	Practitioner	Who rejected it?	Who accepted it?	When was it accepted?	What contributions evolved black sacred music/gospel music?
Quartet sub-genre.	Dixie Hummingbirds Soul Stirrers Pilgrim Travelers Highway QCs	The mainline black churches.	C.O.G.I.C Pentecostal Holiness Sanctified churches. Non-church venues.	During the golden age of gospel starting in the early 1940s.	Practices on crowd engagement, vocal arrangement, and stylist approaches. Flamboyance and décor in appearance. Sermonizing or "preaching" the song.

Development (1920s–1930s) and Traditional Gospel Era (1930–1945)
Influences on the Evolution of the Gospel Music Industry
A Compilation of Contributions in Art Form, Practices (Industry/Ministry), and Venues

Table 2-B

Contributor	Art Form	Practices	Venues
Charles Tindley Lucie Campbell	Gospel hymns.	*Industry:* Publications of music. Singer-preacher artist (Tindley). Influence provided exposure (Campbell). *Ministry:* Music eventually accepted in the Black Church/compiled in *Gospel Pearls* for worship.	Local church, concerts/services outside of morning worship. Conferences/National Baptist Convention.
Thomas Dorsey (Composer)	Gospel music, fusion with blues.	*Industry:* Created and promoted a gospel circuit/paid concert. Artist development. Music publications. Prolific songwriter (sacred and secular). Recording artist. *Ministry:* Teaching and developing others (NCGCC). Psalmist.	Community concerts. Local church. Conferences/conventions. Touring.

Contributor	Art Form	Practices	Venues
Sallie Martin (Soloist) Roberta Martin (Soloist)	Vocalist.	*Industry:* Martin and Morris Publishing (S. Martin). Live demonstration. *Ministry:* Teaching and developing others (NCGCC). Psalmist.	Community concerts. Local church. Conferences/conventions. Touring.
Kenneth Morris	Organist.	*Industry:* Introduced the Hammond organ in gospel music. Co-founded Martin and Morris Publishing with Sallie Martin. *Ministry:* Broke racial barriers by starting a black-owned-and-operated publishing company that helped propel music career for black and white clients.	The local church, the community, and the industry.
Rosetta Thorpe (Guitarist/Singer/Writer)	Traditional gospel.	*Industry:* The first gospel singer to sign to a major commercial company called Decca Records. *Ministry:* She took the gospel to nightclubs. Luke 14:23 NKJV "Go out into the highways and hedges, and compel them to come in, that my house may be filled."	Concerts. Clubs (Cotton Club).

Golden Age of Gospel (1945 to Mid-1960s)
(1960–1967 Modern Traditional Included)
Post-World War II

In summary, the golden age of gospel exemplified an established and accepted genre of traditional gospel that unfolded various styles that were fully accepted in the Black Church. It also flourished outside the church and had established a sustainable gospel music industry. Thus, the problem statement continues to apply, and Table 3-B at the end of this section captures the evidence of the issue. It also compiles examples of how ministry still took place alongside the demands of the industry.

The support for the hypothesis is illustrated on Figure 3 at the end of this section. It shows the continuum with adaptations between the gospel music from the developmental and traditional era to the golden age of gospel. Negro spirituals, gospel hymnody, Protestant hymns, and now gospel songs were sung by jubilee quartet groups. They eventually adapted their a cappella style to include instrumentation and the sound evolved from university jubilee to the "folk"-style gospel tradition, with some influence of Pentecostal singing, which was not initially favored in the Protestant churches.

The support for the hypothesis is outlined in Table 3-A. As the venue for singing outside the church flourished with the gospel highway, so did the acceptance of varied styles. Initially black males sang quartet and females were not regularly engaged. However, another adaptation was the sound created by all-female groups like the Caravans and the Clara Ward Singers. Roberta Martin took this blend a step further and became the first to mix male and female voices in an ensemble. These practices set a trend that provided a new opportunity for the next generation of gospel singers. Black churches that initially rejected gospel music in the developmental era (1920s–1930s) now wanted a part of the action as gospel choirs recorded and flourished. Many of these were community or conference choirs influenced by the work of Mattie Moss Clark and James Cleveland. The popularity of the gospel choir became a staple in the Black Church.

Figure 3 Continuum of Gospel Music (Golden Age/Modern Contemporary)

Traditional → **Golden Age** → **Modern Contemporary**

Traditional
- Traditional gospel music birthed from urban influence
- Blues fusion
- Thomas Dorsey
- Sallie Martin
- Mahalia Jackson
- Stylistic variations in quartet
  - 1930–1945

Golden Age
- Folk gospel-style quartet flourishes
- Jackson Southernaires, Mighty Clouds of Joy
- Added instrumentaiton
- Ensembles flourished, Clara Ward Singers, Roberta Martin Singers
- Recorded choirs emerged with James Cleveland and Mattie Moss-Clark
- Mahalia Jackson was queen of gospel

- 1945–mid-1960s
- Modern traditional: 1960–1967

Modern Contemporary
- Freedom songs of civil rights
- Message music by the Staple Singers
- Cleveland influences ensembles and intermixes secular lyrics
- Rearranged hymns by choirs/groups
- Pop, rock traditional, country, influences by Andraé Crouch
- Edwin Hawkins, Walter Hawkins add classical/jazz
- "O Happy Day" crossover
- Shirley Caesar evangelizes songs
- Late 1960s–1970s

Golden Age of Gospel (1945–Mid-1960s)
(1960–1967 Modern Traditional Included)
Gospel Music Social Acceptance vs. Evolution of Gospel Music

Table 3-A

What was controversial or rejected? When did it occur?	Practitioner	Who rejected it?	Who accepted it?	When was it accepted?	What contributions evolved black sacred music/gospel music?
Pentecostal-style practices in the singing of early quartet groups. (Jubilee style was accepted by Protestant blacks.)	Early folk-style quartet groups.	Mainline black churches.	C.O.G.I.C Pentecostal Holiness Sanctified churches. Non-church venues.	During the golden age of gospel starting in the early 1940s.	Practices on crowd engagement, vocal arrangement, and stylist approaches. Flamboyance and décor in appearance. Sermonizing or evangelizing the song.

Golden Age of Gospel (1945–Mid-1960s)
(1960–1967 Modern Traditional Included)
Influences on the Evolution of the Gospel Music Industry
A Compilation of Contributions in Art Form, Practices (Industry/Ministry), and Venues

Table 3-B

Contributors	Art Form	Practices	Venues
Folk gospel-style quartet groups. Jackson Southernaires Mighty Clouds of Joy	Folk gospel style quartet music.	*Industry:* Regional groups gained celebrity with supported income. Influenced secular genres. Quartet singing became a sustainable format in gospel. *Ministry:* Became an empowering brotherhood for black men during an era of social injustice.	Gospel highway (outside the church). Radio. Television.
Ensembles Clara Ward Singers, Roberta Martin Singers, Sallie Martin Singers, Caravans	Traditional and contemporary for the era of gospel singing. Some female quartets.	*Industry:* Open doors for new venues for gospel music such as secular TV, more radio presence. Ensemble singing became a staple in gospel. *Ministry:* Empowered black women during era of social injustice.	Church. Community. Television. Gospel highway. Radio.
Mattie Moss Clark/ James Cleveland	Gospel choir music.	*Industry:* Sustainable recording choirs. *Ministry:* Raised the standard for choir singing. Opened doors for community and mass choirs.	Church. Community. Radio. Conferences.

Contemporary Period (Late 1960s–1970s)
(1967– Present Often Referred to as the Modern Contemporary Era)
Civil Rights Movement and Post-Civil Rights Eras

In summary, the contemporary era (1960s–1970s) was an era when many more groups joined the gospel music scene and distinct stylistic changes occurred. There were more opportunities for exposure through television shows, the availability of more record players in black homes, and radio airplay. The key elements of this era align with the hypothesis as illustrated in Figure 4 at the end of this section. Continuity exists from the golden age (1945– 1965) and the modern traditional (1960s–1967) to the contemporary era (late 1960s–1970s). This is demonstrated by the continuation of sermonizing or evangelizing the music, initially started by the quartets of the golden age. More female quartets such as the Truthettes emerged, while the traditional male quartet groups continued to thrive. Shirley Caesar became well known for this technique, especially in her solo career. Hymns were still a staple of gospel music yet were reworked and rearranged by choirs, soloists, and ensembles—one example of an adaptation on the continuum.

Another adaptation that initially met with controversy was the stylistic changes introduced by Crouch and Hawkins that modernized the musical sound by fusing in elements of classical, pop, jazz, blues, country, and soul. This created more crossover appeal that attracted other races and secular audiences. Hawkins was criticized by the Black Church when "O Happy Day," a re-arranged hymn, created a demand for him to sing in secular venues such as nightclubs. At the time, this was not an acceptable venue for gospel artists. Theses controversies are outlined in Table 4A at the end of this section. The problem statement continued to be evident as the practitioners of this era were challenged not to appear "too worldly" and still were able to leverage the controversies and business aspects of the industry to do ministry.

Figure 4: Continuum of Gospel Music (Modern Contemporary and New Millennium)

Modern Contemporary Modern Contemporary  New Millennium

Modern Contemporary
- Freedom songs of civil rights
- Message music by the Staple Singers
- Cleveland influences ensembles and intermixes secular lyrics
- Rearranged hymns by choirs/groups
- Pop, rock, traditional, country influences by Andraé Crouch
- Edwin Hawkins, Walter Hawkins add classical/jazz
- "O Happy Day" crossover
- Shirley Caesar evangelizes songs
- Late 1960s–1970s

Modern Contemporary
- Crouch precedes CCM and the Word music movement
- Traditional artists seek relevance: Williams Bros, Rance Allen, Shirley Caesar
- Winans and Commissioned
- Jazz, R&B, hip-hop influence
- Hezekiah Walker, John P. Kee, Thompson Community, Wilmington Chester, Tri-City, Sounds of Blackness, Richard Smallwood
- Virtuoso singing of the Clark Sisters, Vanessa Bell Armstrong, Daryl Coley, Tramaine Hawkins
- Young urban sound emerges.
- Jazz artists emerge: Ben Tankard, Allen/Allen, Whitfield
- More crossover appeal from Kirk Franklin, William Becton, BeBe and CeCe Winans, Mary Mary
- 1980s–1990s

New Millennium
- Kirk Franklin revolution
- Mary Mary
- Israel Houghton
- Yolanda Adams
- BeBe Winans
- CeCe Winans
- Ricky Dillard
- Jay Moss
- Kiarra Sheard
- Ty Tribette
- Tasha Cobbs
- Cross Movement
- Lacrae
- Da Truth
- Canton Jones
- 2000–2015

Modern Contemporary (late 1960s–1970s)/(1980s–1990s)
Gospel Music Social Acceptance vs. Evolution of Gospel Music

Table 4-A

What was controversial or rejected? When did it occur?	Practitioner	Who rejected it?	Who accepted it?	When was it accepted?	What contributions evolved black sacred music/gospel music?
Gospel music was rejected in college music departments because it was not viewed as "serious" and did not display the standard aesthetic. (1960s)	Black gospel musicians who were formally and classically trained.	College music departments. HBCUs and traditional white schools. Formally trained musicians.	Black college students who played and sang gospel music.	When black students insisted on curriculum changes to recognize it. Richard Smallwood organized the gospel choir at Howard Univ. in 1965.	Classical influence in gospel music became appreciated in the church, community, and industry. Gospel renditions of classical songs and hymns evolved.
Crossover music, emergence in appearance, further fusion of musical style/instrumentation. (Late 1960s– 1970s)	Edwin Hawkins Hawkins Singers (appearance) Andraé Crouch	The Black Church community rejected the practice of crossover in gospel.	Contemporary music moved into Presbyterian, Episcopal, and Catholic churches.	When gospel music became cross-cultural and cross-denominational.	Hawkins and Crouch introduced a new contemporary sound with jazz/R&B influence as demonstrated in "O Happy Day."
Gospel artists collaborating in secular venues with secular appeal and further crossover music. (1980s–1990s)	The Winans Commissioned Yolanda Adams K. Franklin W. Becton Mary Mary	The Black Church community rejected the practice of crossover in gospel and secular appeal.	Non-church venues. Young generation.	Ten years later post-Kirk Franklin revolution.	Contemporary urban genre. Christian contemporary.

Modern Contemporary (late 1960s–1970s)/(1980s–1990s) Influences on the Evolution of the Gospel Music Industry
A Compilation of Contributions in Art Form, Practices (Industry/Ministry), and Venues

Table 4-B

Contributor	Art Form	Practices	Venues
James Cleveland	Traditional gospel music.	*Industry:* Producing live recording of gospel choirs. Remaking secular songs as gospel. *Ministry:* Producing numerous groups at Savoy Records and launching careers.	Community. Industry.
Mahalia Jackson	Traditional gospel music.	*Industry:* First gospel celebrity and entrepreneur. *Ministry:* Used stardom for civil rights movement.	International presence. Social Justice and Political Scene. Television. Industry.
Richard Smallwood	Contemporary gospel music.	*Industry:* Classical influence in gospel music. *Ministry:* Acceptance of gospel music in academia.	Academia. Community. Industry.
Hawkins Crouch The Winans (BeBe and CeCe) Commissioned Kirk Franklin John P. Kee William Becton Yolanda Adams Mary Mary	Urban contemporary. Christian contemporary.	*Industry:* New trends in contemporary gospel music, evolution of urban contemporary, evolution of Christian contemporary. More trends in cross-cultural, cross-genre, crossover styles.	More venues for gospel music: Various TV programs. Theme parks. Awards shows. Industry. Sacred meets secular.

Modern Contemporary (1980s-1990 /1990s-2000)
Emerging Trends in Gospel Music,
Gospel Music Business and Sound

In summary, the contemporary era (1980s–1990s) up to 2000 demonstrated an expansion in subgenres for gospel music including new traditional, urban contemporary, inspirational, Christian contemporary, jazz, and hip-hop. The key elements of this era align with the hypothesis illustrated in Figure 4, referred to in the prior section. The continuum from the 1960s–1970s when compared with 1980s–1990s and up to 2000 shows an expansion of the contemporary sound launched by Hawkins and Crouch to more groups, with stylistic variations and more artists with crossover appeal in music, appearance, and practices. For example, the jazz and classical influence of Hawkins continues with artists like Thomas Whitfield and Richard Smallwood. Crouch's and Hawkins's influence is evident in the contemporary instrumentation style of the Winans and Commissioned as they were liberated to continue with greater acceptance in their decade. Crouch paved the way for BeBe and CeCe Winans to be accepted in the predominantly white CCM genre, with the multicultural appeal he illustrated with the Disciples. The virtuoso-style singing demonstrated by Vanessa Bell Armstrong and the Clark Singers continued with artists like Yolanda Adams and Kim Burrell, who would eventually adapt the sound with jazz and R&B elements. Hawkins and Crouch were supported by the young generation, which was attracted to their sound and look. The social acceptance of gospel artists not in robes and having more mainstream looks and sounds was an adaptation that continued in the artists of the 1980s and 1990s and beyond. Table 4-A outlines the controversy and Table 4-B shows evidence of the problem. These practitioners managed to continue ministering while in the industry, per the examples shown.

Kirk Franklin, who does not claim to be a singer, reinvented the practice of "evangelizing" the song, or even the old practice of "lining" a hymn that took place before the 1900s. He "talked" the lead part of *The Reason Why We Sing* as the "front man" of the Family. This was an adaptation to the practice seen by traditional groups, who often were great singers and sang it instead of spoke it. He gave new meaning to being the "exalter" in gospel music. With *The Reason Why We Sing*, Kirk Franklin and the Family continued the traditional vocals, with modern traditional musical arrangements and some contemporary. It was not until the release of *Stomp* that Franklin's display of youthful dancing to a secular sample mixed by funk group Parliament and his hip-hop style appearance became an issue. His urbanization of gospel and collaboration with secular artists was initially met with controversy. As history showed with Dorsey and others to follow, Franklin would introduce the next major "revolution" in gospel music.

Gospel Music in the New Millennium (2000-2015)

In summary, the contemporary era from 2000 to 2015, the new millennium, when compared with music from the 1980s to the 1990s, continued to demonstrate an expansion in subgenres for gospel music that included new traditional, urban contemporary, inspirational, Christian contemporary, jazz, and hip-hop. The key elements of this era align with the hypothesis as outlined in Figure 4 in the prior section and Table 5-A at the end of this section.

For example, praise and worship made a new impact on the Black Church as we entered the new millennium. This demonstrates continuity in gospel music, as an adaptation to the congregational and devotional-style singing that took root in black sacred music from the Pentecostal movement and serves the same purpose as gospel hymnody in the early 1900s. The concept to have simple repetitive call-and-response-style songs was a continued practice that actually started with folk spirituals and slaves' prayer meetings. For the Black Church, as the choir took center stage at church and the congregations became observers, the concept of congregational singing as primary was untapped for decades in most black churches. Praise and worship was an adaptation of this concept. When it was introduced in white churches as a genre in the 1990s, the use of praise teams and worship leaders appeared to be a threat to the purpose of the choir. Megachurches, which had masses of unchurched people who did not know hymns and gospel music, often preferred a praise band to the choir. The concept of a praise team was initially rejected by black churches until they saw the concept in practice and demonstrated by other churches. Integrating this into a traditional style service continues to be a challenge today for black churches. It seems to be in place in some churches because it is a trend and not because it is effective.

The rise of hip-hop in gospel music is a continuation of the contemporary urban influence initiated by the young generation that followed John P. Kee, Hezekiah Walker, and Kirk Franklin. It was met initially with rejection in gospel music circles because of the secular similarities in musical style and appearance. Hip-hop continues to demonstrate the trend of crossover appeal. The music of Lecrae has even transcended the *Billboard* charts and has outstanding sales in non-Christian genres.

The urbanization of gospel music and cross collaboration in secular and sacred efforts demonstrated by artists discussed in this section initially caused their struggle for acceptance in the Black Church community. However, as their forerunners like Dorsey, Clara Ward, Rosetta Thorpe, Hawkins, and Crouch showed, new venues outside the church would support the art form and offer an opportunity to reach more people with the message. As an example, Franklin paved the way for Mary Mary, Da Truth, Canton Jones, and Lacrae, while CeCe Winans paved the way for Yolanda Adams, Kim Burrell, and artists to come.

The problem statement is more evident as the continuum progresses to the present time, as shown in Table 5-B. Artists managed to leverage the competitive nature of the music industry, not just the gospel music industry, to conduct ministry.

Modern Contemporary, New Millennium (2000-2015)
Gospel Music Social Acceptance vs. Evolution of Gospel Music

Table 5-A

What was controversial or rejected? When did it occur?	Practitioner	Who rejected it?	Who accepted it?	When was it accepted?	What contributions evolved black sacred music/gospel music?
Praise and worship genre in black churches.	Israel Houghton Donnie McClurkin Kurt Karr Martha Mannuzzi Vicki Yohee	The Black Church community.	CCM audience. Megachurches.	When black gospel artists released black renditions of praise and worship songs or original praise and worship songs. White artists release praise and worship with gospel appeal.	Black praise and worship artists emerged and have sustained a presence in gospel music.
Gospel music and performances with radically strong secular and urban appeal. Collaboration with secular artists and secular venues. Christian hip-hop.	Yolanda Adams Kirk Franklin Mary Mary Da Truth Ty Tribette Canton Jones Lacrae	The Black Church community.	Non-church venues. The young generation.	When Kirk Franklin collaborated with traditional gospel artists (Shirley Caesar/ Lee Williams/ Rance Allen). Kirk Franklin became an icon in the music industry, setting the stage for others.	Artists with crossover, cross-genre, and secular appeal can chart and compete in non-gospel categories on *Billboard*, Grammys, and other secular industry award academies. Gospel artists can leverage the secular opportunities to spread the gospel.

Modern Contemporary Millennium (2000-2015)
Influences on the Evolution of the Gospel Music Industry
A Compilation of Contributions in Art Form, Practices (Industry/Ministry), and Venues

Table 5-B

Contributor	Art Form	Practices	Venues
Kirk Franklin	Contemporary urban gospel. Gospel TV competition.	*Industry:* Revolutionized the production in quality of gospel music, raised the standard for how record labels planned market budgets, raised the standard in live performance and touring, leveraged collaboration with secular artists to bridge the gap between sacred and secular venues. Powerbroker in the industry (radio, TV, producers, artists). *Ministry:* Artist United for Haiti (relief effort). Introduced and produced numerous artists to the industry. Preacher of the gospel. Venues and music that targets the youth and unchurched/openly shares his testimony via books and preaching engagements.	International reach. Concerts in auditoriums/arenas. Industry. Church and non-church venues.
LeCrae	Christian hip-hop.	*Industry:* Music is crossover. Bridges sacred and secular. *Ministry:* RealLife Ministries *This Is Fatherhood* initiative.	

Field Experience

I completed a series of field experiences from 2011 to 2015 in the form of interviews, conferences, seminars, training, and observations in these settings. A full list of these is included in the bibliography. The outputs of these activities are interjected where appropriate in the research. Response papers were compiled as an account of the experience on each activity and can be obtained from me for review. The objective of attending these events was to obtain a breadth of knowledge about the African-American worship experience for practical applications. Gospel artists need to be familiar with the hymnal process so this can be a way to distribute songs targeted for church worship. All the authors were aspiring composers at some point. There are composers included who are not on mainstream radio.

African-American Church Music Seminars

Seminars helped me broaden my knowledge of black hymnody, spirituals, and homiletics. Dr. James Abbington is a primary scholar in this area and periodically conducts hymnal seminars to demonstrate hymns, as Dorsey did with Sallie Martin. The songs range from hymns that depict the early African-American church scene to modern-day worship styles, both traditional and contemporary. There were also selections chosen to fit different segments of a typical worship service or different types of services.

When the Black Church was birthed, European influence in the worship style did not destroy all evidence of Africanism. Hymnals and spiritual songs of the Black Church are found in *Readings in African-American Church Music and Worship,* compiled and edited by African-American church music scholar James Abbington.

The *Total Praise* hymnal, compiled in 2011 by GIA Publications, is a contemporary collection of hymns, spirituals, anthems, and spirituals representative of the Black Church. Dr. James Abbington has been instrumental in providing a live demonstration and interpretation of select hymns from the *Total Praise* collection. He has travelled the nation conducting seminars to provide a sampling of the songs and to exhibit the interpretation.

"Old-church" worship, as this style is affectionately called in the African-American church community, is characterized by the old gospel piano flow, syncopation, long notes, and sweet soulful harmonies. Dr. Abbington reminded the participants of the birth of gospel music by one of the founding fathers, Thomas Dorsey, in the 1930s. One of the hymns reviewed was #572, called "I Do, Don't You?" (GIA Publications, 2011). The interpretation Dr. Abbington shared was one of free style and with ad lib, which is characteristic of African-American improvisation styles. Dorsey is most known for his hymn "Precious Lord, Take My Hand," Hymn #478, (GIA Publications, 2011), which he wrote after hearing of the death of his wife and newborn child (Dr. James Abbington, personal communication, August 27, 2011).

One of the composers from the contemporary era included in *Total Praise* (GIA Publications, 2011) is Walter Hawkins from the infamous Hawkins Family. Hymn #197, "Jesus Christ Is the Way," is one of Hawkins's most popular compositions (Dr. James Abbington, personal communication, August 27, 2011).

Total Praise (GIA Publications, 2011) is a unique hymnal in that it covers a broad range and style of traditional hymns and gospel, as well as contemporary gospel and praise and worship songs. Hymn #371, "He's Blessing Me," is a song by Norris Garner, a modern-day composer who captures traditional style. I have had the pleasure of working with him as a vocalist in an ensemble he had while in Raleigh before relocating to California.

There are gospel artists in the *Total Praise* who currently have recordings in circulation on radio airplay and on the Internet. These include #179, "Now Behold the Lamb," by modern-day king of gospel Kirk Franklin; #333, "I Need You to Survive," by Hezekiah Walker; #321, "How Great Is Our God," by Chris Tomlin; #104, "In the Sanctuary," by Kurt Carr; and #109, "Praise Him in Advance," by Deon Kipping (Dr. James Abbington, personal communication, August 27, 2011, and GIA Publications, 2011).

Gospel Music One Sound Project

> The hope of this project is to bring the church music ministry and the gospel music industry to one accord, ONE SOUND, spiritually and in the natural (technically and physically) for Kingdom building.
>
> – Antonia Arnold-McFarland
> *See 2 Chronicles 5:13–14*

The Gospel Music One Sound Project was a comprehensive effort from November 1–23, 2015, launched to compile a focus group for the exchange of dialogue online, to provide awareness of gospel music history, and to capture challenges in music ministry in the local church, community, and gospel music industry. Two research instruments were executed by a Survey Monkey link on the Gospel Music One Sound Project Facebook page. These provided rigor for an analysis specific to the problem statement and hypothesis and for the practical needs of local church and community music ministry.

Instructional posts and videos were distributed by Facebook explaining the purpose and approach of the project. The intervention was conducted over three weeks with specific activities, along with posts targeted at engaging online conversations addressed to the problem statement, hypothesis, and practical needs in the local church music ministry.

In week one, on November 3, 2015, the Gospel Music One Sound pre-test collector was launched. It consisted of 28 participations. They completed the 31-question survey for baseline data on demographics and specific questions aimed at their thoughts and opinions on the problem statement and hypothesis. In weeks two and three, dialogue on current topics in ministry and industry continued. I also hosted and facilitated two webinars featuring Professor L. Stanley Davis in lecture style on *Chicago's Roots in Gospel Music*.

Also in week two I conducted a survey called "Music Ministry Development," targeted at identifying issues faced by local church and community music ministries. Although the focus of this study was from the perspective of independent gospel artists in balancing ministry and industry, their role in the local church is often very much a part of the ministry work they do. Most gospel artists have at some point been part of a local church music ministry and have to balance their involvement with time dedicated to gospel industry pursuits. There were 29 anonymous participants who completed 17 questions. The survey was posted on the Facebook page and circulated by email to my musician and pastoral contacts in African-American churches in the Raleigh-Durham area. They had various roles in the church music ministry, including spiritual advising as a minister or pastor. The church sizes were primarily 300 members or fewer, one service per Sunday, and included the youth choir, male choir, adult mixed-voice or mass choir, and a praise team.

In week three the onsite seminar and concert provided more awareness of social acceptance of art form, practice, and venues in the evolution of gospel music. It took place at Oak City Baptist Church in Raleigh and included national gospel artist and pastor William Becton as the lead clinician. On day one of the seminar (November 20) I provided a brief knowledge leveling on Gospel Music One Sound and introduced the SWOT analysis as a tool that can be used to address practical issues in music ministry. This is demonstrated in Tables 9-A and 9-B for my music ensemble Blessed Union, The Group. Approximately 25 attendees worked individually or in groups to compile a SWOT analysis for personal, church, or group music ministry pursuits. Several participants presented their findings and potential solutions for their weaknesses and threats.

We referenced 2 Chronicles 5:13–14 as the vision for the ultimate worship experience in the church, the community, and the industry. The name of the intervention effort of Gospel Music One Sound stems from this scripture. This was also the scripture Pastor Becton used as a basis in teaching awareness of biblical foundations in music ministry.

> Indeed it came to pass, when the trumpeters and singers *were* as one, to make one sound to be heard in praising and thanking the LORD, and when they lifted up their voice with the trumpets and cymbals and instruments of music, and praised the LORD, *saying:*
>
> "*For He is* good,
> For His mercy *endures* forever,"
>
> that the house, the house of the LORD, was filled with a cloud, so that the priests could not continue ministering because of the cloud; for the glory of the LORD filled the house of God.
> – 2 Chronicles 5:13–14 NKJV

On the morning of day two there was a panel discussion by industry and ministry experts on the issues identified in both survey instruments. These are compiled in Tables 10, 11-A, and 11-B at the end of this section and present the challenges faced by practitioners of gospel music in the church and community and as independent artists pursuing the gospel music industry. The Music Ministry Development Survey consisted of 29 participants.

In the evening of day two we held a free concert in the form of a learning and worship experience. It was a live performance to demonstrate the gospel music timeline. It included praise dance, live music, big-screen visual aids, and a skit as another approach to investigate the hypothesis. Dialogue and one-on-one interviews were collected to gauge social acceptance of the worship arts practices used in the concert. The Gospel Music One Sound post-test collector was launched with the same questions as the pre-test. A total of 23 participants completed this survey from November 21 to 23. Quantitative results and findings of the data are outlined in the following pages.

As shown in Tables 6 and 7, the participants of the pre-test and post-test surveys were 76.2% female, 23.8% male, 100% African-American, and approximately 95% ages 39–60, which is Generation X and Baby Boomer Group 2. Approximately 35% of the participants affiliated with a Baptist association and approximately 2% identified as Christian non-denominational.

The participants could choose multiple answers on several questions about their preferred styles of gospel music, the styles most prevalent in their gospel group or church music ministry, and the roles they play in the gospel music landscape. A sample of these "check all that apply" questions is shown in Table 12. This is a representative of how data was cross-tabulated for meaningful trends. This depiction shows that for the 28 pre-test participants, traditional gospel music tends to be the preferred style at their churches. This correlates to the fact that most of the participants were Baptist, Generation X, and Baby Boomers. The historical analysis revealed that the Baptist denomination early on was more conservative in musical appeal.

Most of the participants held a leadership position in their local church music ministry as choir directors, worship leaders, praise team members, musicians, ministers of music, or music directors. Most also participated in local, regional, or national music organizations and were serving in community groups or performing as independent artists.

Across the board the 14 questions to find opinions on the problem statement and hypothesis shown in Table 8 show a favorable trend toward more support after intervention with dialogue, webinars, seminars, and the concert. Table 8 shows the percent change in response between the pre-test and post-test surveys. A positive number indicates an increase in responses and a negative indicates a decrease. Questions 14, 16, 18, 19, 20, 21, 22, 24, and 25 indicate some form of an increase in agreement with the statement. For example, in question 14 the number of responders who strongly agree that they are very aware of the history of gospel music and how it has evolved since its birth in the 1930s increased by 13.1%.

Questions 19–23 show a favorable trend toward social acceptance of gospel music and artists engaging in secular platforms as an opportunity for ministry. As the review of the literature indicates, gospel music and artists in the new millennium are using their celebrity to bridge the gap between sacred and secular and focusing on taking their message to new territory and in new formats such as reality television, music competitions, radio, and even prayer meetings before NBA games.

Questions 24 and 25 are good examples that capture the essence of the hypothesis. I believe the history lesson activities with the webinar and the skit in the concert played a role in demonstrating an increase in confidence in opinion. Question 24 indicates a 13.1% increase in strong agreement and 16.7% in agreement that, without compromising the message, Kirk Franklin liberated gospel music and "broke the chains" that have held it to limited appeal and exposure. The 17.9% increase in strong agreement in question 25 spells out that hip-hop is on the rise in Christian music and that the participants had a better understanding after the intervention activities on the trend of controversy in the history of gospel music.

I attended the 2011 Perfecting Music Conference for two days in Charlotte, which was hosted by Donnie McClurkin. It included various seminars for ministry and industry knowledge that were conducted by gospel artists, radio personalities, and industry personnel. A compilation of best practices for aspiring gospel artists has been compiled as qualitative data in Table 13. These findings were provided by industry artists and professionals who have demonstrated their expertise.

Table 6
Gospel Music One Sound PrePost Test Demographics

Gender	
Male	23.8%
Female	76.2%
Total	**100%**

Ethnicity	
African-American/Black	100%
Caucasian American/White	0%
Hispanic/Latino	0%
Asian/Pacific Islander	0%
Native American	0%
Other (please specify)	0%
Total	**100%**

Age Group	
13–20 (Gen Z) No participants are allowed under age 13	0.0%
21–28 (Generation Y/ Millenniums)	4.8%
39–49 (Generation X)	52.4%
50–60 (Baby Boomers 2)	42.9%
61–69 (Baby Boomers 1)	0.0%
70–87 (Post-War Cohorts)	0.0%
88 and above	0.0%
Total	**100%**

Location	
Raleigh, North Carolina	100%

Table 7 Denominations	
African Methodist Episcopal Church (A.M.E.)	0.0%
African Methodist Episcopal Zion Church (A.M.E.Z.)	0.0%
Christian Methodist Episcopal (C.M.E, formerly Colored Methodist Episcopal)	0.0%
United Methodist (UMC)	0.0%
The National Baptist Convention, U.S.A., Incorporated (N.B.C.)/The National Baptist Convention of America, Unincorporated (N.B.C.A.)/The Progressive National Baptist Convention (P.N.B.C.)	28.6%
National Association of Freewill Baptists	4.8%
Full Gospel Baptist Church Fellowship International	0.0%
The Church of God in Christ (C.O.G.I.C.)	4.8%
Presbyterian Church (USA)	0.0%
United Church of Christ	9.5%
International Pentecostal Holiness Church (IPHC)	0.0%
Christian Church (Disciples of Christ)	0.0%
Apostolic Assembly/Apostolic Pentecostal	4.8%
Non-denominational Christian affiliation	23.8%
Independent denominational Protestant (Baptist, Christian Church)	14.3%
National Black Catholic Congress/Other Catholic affiliation	0.0%
Other (please specify)	9.5%
Answers for Other	
Missionary Baptist, Pentecostal	
Total	**100%**

Table 8		Pre- and Post- Test Trend of Change				
Number	Survey Statement	5) Strongly Agree	4) Agree	3) Neutral	2) Disagree	1) Strongly Disagree
14	I am very aware of the history of gospel music and how it has evolved since its birth in the 1930s.	13.1%	20.3%	-26.2%	-3.6%	-3.6%
15	I believe that increasing my awareness in the history of gospel music will help me better understand my role and plan my future in the local church, community, or gospel music industry.	-11.9%	8.3%	7.2%	-3.6%	0.0%
16	What was once viewed as sounding "secular" or "worldly" in musical style, instrumentation, beats, and lyrics eventually becomes acceptable and normal in gospel music.	0.0%	20.3%	-13.1%	-3.6%	-3.6%

Number	Survey Statement	5) Strongly Agree	4) Agree	3) Neutral	2) Disagree	1) Strongly Disagree
17	What was once viewed as looking "secular" or "worldly" in the appearance of gospel artist eventually becomes acceptable and normal.	-4.8%	0.0%	-1.2%	9.5%	-3.6%
18	Thomas Dorsey used blues / jazz progressions in the development of gospel music, causing it to be rejected initially.	17.9%	27.4%	-27.3%	-14.3%	-3.6%
19	Kirk Franklin is able to use the business aspect of the music industry to the advantage of spreading the gospel, without compromising the message.	9.5%	-4.7%	-6.0%	1.2%	0.0%

Number	Survey Statement	5) Strongly Agree	4) Agree	3) Neutral	2) Disagree	1) Strongly Disagree
20	When gospel songs like "O Happy Day" (Edwin Hawkins), "Stomp" (Kirk Franklin and God's Property) and "Be Encouraged" (William Becton) cross over to secular radio and clubs, this is an advancement for gospel music as ministry.	-3.5%	17.8%	0.0%	-14.3%	0.0%
21	Gospel artists/celebrity pastors who are on reality TV shows build their appeal and brand in the industry, while they use entertainment to demonstrate Christian principles.	3.6%	7.2%	-11.9%	3.6%	-2.3%
22	Gospel artists/celebrity pastors who are radio personalities use this as an opportunity to build their brand/appeal, while entertaining an audience with Christian commentary.	11.9%	9.6%	-21.4%	0.0%	0.0%
Number	Survey Statement	5) Strongly Agree	4) Agree	3) Neutral	2) Disagree	1) Strongly Disagree

Number	Survey Statement	5) Strongly Agree	4) Agree	3) Neutral	2) Disagree	1) Strongly Disagree
23	Gospel artists, who are disciples of Christ, should not mingle and sing in secular venues such as secular awards shows, clubs nor collaboration with secular artists on tours/music projects. This is viewed as conforming to the world and is not a good way to gain new believers.	4.8%	7.2%	-3.6%	10.7%	-19.1%
24	Without compromising the message, Kirk Franklin liberated gospel music and "broke the chains" that have held it to limited appeal and exposure.	13.1%	16.7%	-27.3%	-2.3%	0.0%

Number	Survey Statement	5) Strongly Agree	4) Agree	3) Neutral	2) Disagree	1) Strongly Disagree
25	In the industry, Christian hip hop appeals to the younger generations, yet due to its secular appeal, it is not widely accepted for Black Church worship service. The "initial church rejection" is a trend in gospel music that started with Dorsey and has continued from the 1930s to today.	17.9%	8.3%	-27.3%	1.2%	0.0%
26	Selecting choir members, lead vocalists, or the praise team based on skill is biblical but too divisive for most churches to handle. This is why volunteer choir is the accepted approach.	10.7%	6.0%	-17.8%	1.2%	0.0%

Number	Survey Statement	5) Strongly Agree	4) Agree	3) Neutral	2) Disagree	1) Strongly Disagree
27	As gospel music becomes more difficult for church music ministries to replicate, the skill sets and preparation need to evolve with the music of the gospel music industry.	13.1%	16.7%	-32.1%	5.9%	-3.6%
28	Ongoing spiritual and technical training of music ministry leaders, musicians, singers, and audio/technical support should be a requirement in the local church. This can be done by attending workshops, bringing in instructors and seeking private study.	7.1%	2.4%	-9.5%	0.0%	0.0%

Table 9-A: SWOT Analysis
Blessed Union, The Group

Strengths	Weaknesses
Comradery among loyal members	Time capacity is small; we are over-committed
Name is locally established with a good reputation	Need business strategy
Group has a unique story	Need artist development plan
Leadership and members demonstrate a heart for helping and building hope in others (align with vision)	Need to improve media/web presence
Leadership has above-average industry experience/knowledge for a local artist	Understaffed for admin/tech support
	More members need industry knowledge
Group members have broad musical taste in R&B, funk, jazz, traditional, and contemporary gospel	Need various live performance song sets
Group appeals to young and midlife adults (Baby Boomers, Gen X and Y)	Lack of consistency in commitment
	Need to improve operations plan
Published music has strong radio appeal	
Tech-savvy and administrative skill sets exist in the group, along with musical skills and a network of influence	

Opportunities	Threats
Digital singles on CD Baby and other online marketplaces	Founders need successors
Access to industry professionals and organizations	Need back-up plan for all personnel
Have small core and extended alumni members for performances and for creating own venues	Unexpected health crisis
	Unexpected financial crisis
Groups appeal can be leveraged to niche market in look and sound (similar to Staple Singers, Sounds of Blackness)	Unmanaged personality dynamics
Industry pursuits can be leveraged more for outreach ministry	Need to better understand legal risks

Table 9-B: SWOT Matrix

Blessed Union, The Group	Strengths (Internal)	Weaknesses (Internal)
Opportunities (External)	**What opportunities can be leveraged by strengths?** Leverage outreach experience for industry opportunities that align. Leverage skill sets in group for technical and administrative needs to operate.	**What weaknesses need to be overcome to pursue opportunities?** A planned season calendar will help members plan dedicated time to focus more on group pursuits.
Threats (External)	**How can strengths reduce risk of threats?** Leverage comradery, loyalty, and network of influence to encourage members to have health and wellness plans and do fundraising to offset group expenses.	**What is the plan to prevent weaknesses from being influenced by threats?** Leverage access to industry professionals to increase knowledge in legal risk, authorizations, ramifications, and financial budget for business plans.

Table 10: Quantitative Survey Results (see Table 16 in Appendix 1 for Qualitative)

Music Ministry Development

What challenges hinder the growth of your music ministry/worship arts? Check all that apply.		
Answer Options	**Response Percent**	**Response Count**
Finding musical staff that will stay long term (five years or more).	24.1%	7
Being able to get rid of musical staff members not willing to grow with the ministry.	13.8%	4
Finding the right skill set to help the music ministry grow.	37.9%	11
The minister of music/music director/staff musicians do not have a good relationship with the pastor.	3.4%	1
Setting a budget that will retain the right skill sets for the music.	44.8%	13
Need to improve on equipment, sound system, microphones, instruments, and tools for execution.	27.6%	8
Too much reliance on volunteer support without developing others.	24.1%	7
Competition among the choirs, choir members, musicians, and church leaders.	13.8%	4
No succession planning in leadership of the music ministry to continue when people leave.	27.6%	8

Choir members participate in various other ministries with overlapping commitments.	48.3%	14
Budget does not include additional seminars for choir members.	41.4%	12
Exposing choir members to vocal development. seminars, etc. outside of rehearsal time.	65.5%	19
No vision or plan for growth in the music ministry.	37.9%	11
Lack of capabilities within the music ministry to meet the expectations of the choir.	10.3%	3
Consistency in choir member participation.	41.4%	12
Getting choir members to practice outside of rehearsal.	62.1%	18
Finding repertoire that is within the capability of the choir.	31.0%	9
Participation and attendance of rehearsal.	34.5%	10
Lack of spiritual growth and immaturity deters participation.	24.1%	7
Lack of spiritual growth affects interest and motivation to grow.	31.0%	9
Lack of strategic planning to grow music ministry support with the church.	20.7%	6
Lack of unity in the choir.	24.1%	7
People in music ministry/worship arts need motivation.	27.6%	8

Need better coordination between music, dance, and media to have more effective delivery.	20.7%	6
Other (please explain).		1
	answered questions	29
	skipped questions	0

Table 11–A: Quantitative Pre- and Post-Test Survey Results

29. The types of issues faced in my music ministry can be categorized this way:

Answer Options	Response Percent	Response Count
Shortage of well-developed skill sets (musicians, vocalists and ministry leaders).	60.7%	17
Lack of spiritual maturity to handle constructive training.	57.1%	16
Lack of commitment by participants.	60.7%	17
Lack of understanding of roles and responsibilities/ protocol and structure.	53.6%	15
Shortage of financial resources to hire sufficient support.	53.6%	15
Lack of awareness among leadership/pastors on relevant strategies for effective music ministry.	42.9%	12
Not applicable to me.	7.1%	2
Other (please specify).	3.6%	1
	answered questions	28
	skipped questions	0

Table 11-B: Quantitative Pre- and Post-Test Survey Results

30. The types of issues I face as a gospel artist (solo or group) are as follows:

Answer Options	Response Percent	Response Count
Shortage of well-developed skill sets (musicians, vocalists and ministry leaders) in my group.	32.1%	9
Shortage of business and administrative support.	28.6%	8
Lack of spiritual maturity to handle growth.	25.0%	7
Lack of commitment by participants.	35.7%	10
Competing agendas within the group.	25.0%	7
Shortage of financial resources to cover expenses.	32.1%	9
Lack of knowledge of the music industry.	39.3%	11
Not applicable to me.	25.0%	7
Other (please specify).	7.1%	2
answered questions		28
skipped questions		0

Table 12 (Pre-Test)

Cross Tabulation: Styles of Gospel Music at Church vs. Age Group of Participants

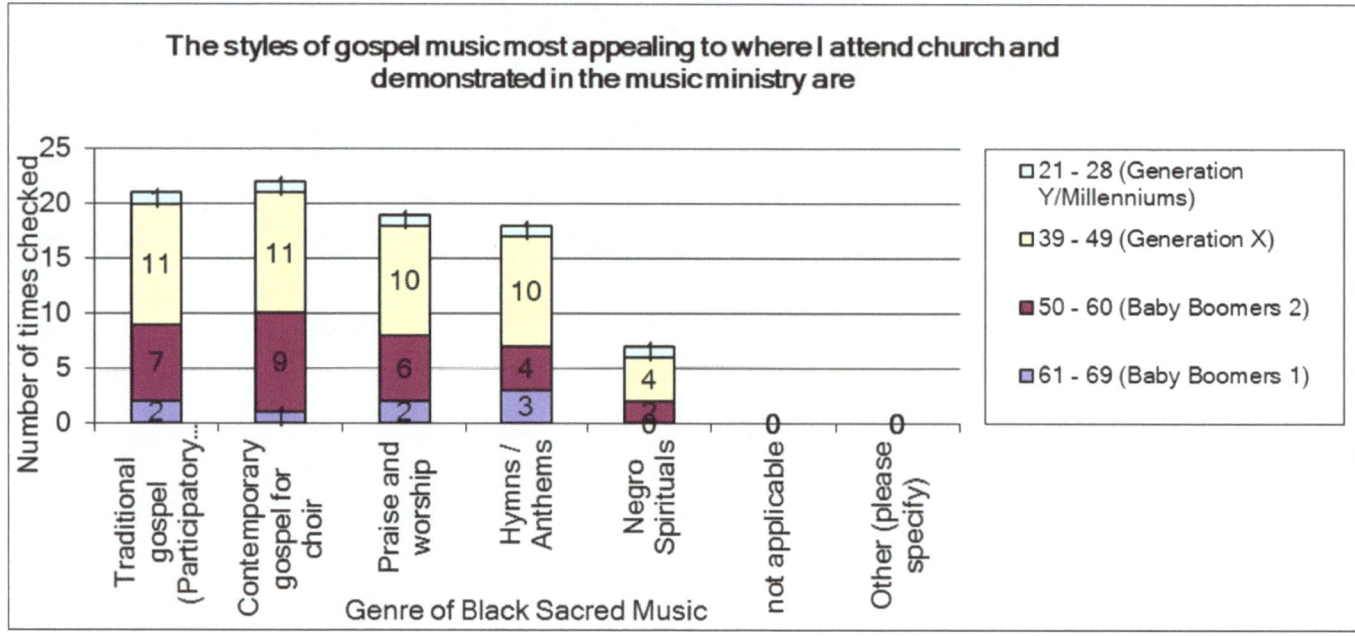

Table 13: Best Practices for Aspiring Gospel Artists, Perfecting Music Conference

Observation or Prescription	Source of Information	Ministry	Industry
The successful gospel artist is effective at creativity, spiritual discernment and maturity, and industry business.	Myron Butler Perfecting Conference 2011	X	X
Ensure legalities for songwriters, collaboration agreements, work-for-hire agreements, copyrights, mechanical license, publications, and producers are established before doing any recordings.	Myron Butler Perfecting Conference 2011		X
Understand clearly record deal points that translate to pay percentages for producers, artists, songwriters, publishers, and record labels. Understand industry standards for publishing compensation when in contract.	Kerry Douglas, Aaron Lindsey Perfecting Conference 2011		X
The best way for new artists to get on the radio is to get traction by having music on the Internet.	Kerry Douglas, Gary Tom Perfecting Conference 2011		X

Observation or Prescription	Source of Information	Ministry	Industry
Artists can build their artist score through social media technology to gain exposure.	Kerry Douglas Perfecting Conference 2011		X
Provide a good live performance in front of large crowds and have music readily available for sale immediately afterward (megachurches, conferences).	Melanie Clark, Israel Houghton Perfecting Conference 2011		X
Life moves at the speed of relationship but not at the speed of opportunity. Great opportunities can follow real relationships. This builds longevity and a legacy.	Aaron Lindsey, Israel Houghton Perfecting Conference 2011	X	
Relationships are the currency of the kingdom. You must be faithful over your local domain before God can trust you with more.	Melanie Clark Perfecting Conference 2011	X	

Observation or Prescription	Source of Information	Ministry	Industry
There is a careful balance of business and ministry in gospel music. Artists or industry participants must be very clear and honest with themselves as to why they are seeking a role in the gospel music industry.	Melanie Clark Perfecting Conference 2011	X	
The gospel artist must be able to effectively deliver a good live performance with a testimony that connects with the audience.	Kerry Douglas Perfecting Conference 2011	X	
As an aspiring gospel artist, each of us must figure out what it is that gets us to that captivating artistic mode.	Conference Concert 2011	X	X
Change the perceptions of musicians in the church by 1) displaying more gratitude, 2) displaying more generosity, 3) having grace, and 4) obtaining godliness from the first 3.	Israel Houghton Perfecting Conference 2011	X	

CHAPTER 6

Summary, Improvements, and Implications of Research Recommendations for Continued Study

Summary

This research began with first establishing a foundational understanding of a theological framework for the study of African-American spirituality. To aid in this, it was important to present the significance of the Black Church to African-Americans and to gain insight into what the African-American worship experience looks like. Three key ingredients in this are the black preacher, the congregation, and the music ministry.

Next, a systematic review of the literature by the scholarly defined eras in the evolution of black sacred music provided insight into the evolution of the African-American worship experience. Then an analysis that consisted of an assessment of the literature and field experience provided quantitative and qualitative results from data collected through two research instruments and ethnographic findings in field experience. Best practices, improvements, and implications were compiled from a comprehensive look at all efforts and activities. The gospel artists often must balance their music ministry as artisst with their involvement in the local church. The results of the music ministry development survey revealed issues faced in the local church music ministry. These questions, issues, and practical applications are compiled in Appendix 1 in Table 16. The ability of artists to manage and lead others through this offers the opportunity to practice how they can manage their individual industry pursuits. There are similarities and key differences in challenges faced. Generally, the church has volunteer participants in the choir while industry groups seek the most skilled. Thus, the expectations of output should not be the same. Gospel artists may need to be versed with repertoire and church music hymnals and anthems so they can operate effectively in this venue.

As an aspiring independent gospel artist (Blessed Union, The Group), I had a personal connection with the problem statement for this study. Findings identified during the assessment of the literature and revealed from the survey results in chapter 5 support the hypothesis. For convenience, the problem statement and hypothesis are presented below:

> The problem is that the independent gospel artist is challenged to balance ministry against the demands of the music industry. As a disciple of Christ, the independent gospel artist is expected to spread the gospel through song, while not compromising or conforming to the conflicting values of the music industry aimed at mainstream cultural appeal. In other words, how does the independent gospel artist balance ministry focus against the demands of the industry and sustain effectiveness without compromising his or her Christian faith?

As a hypothesis, the history of gospel music demonstrates continuity in the elements of gospel music with necessary adaptations in an accepted form from the Dorsey to the Franklin eras. As gospel music has evolved, so has the social acceptance of what was once controversial in art form, practices, and venue. This has liberated the next generation of gospel artists to have greater opportunity for ministry while leveraging the music industry.

Improvements and Control Plan

The resolution of the problem faced by the independent gospel artist on how to effectively balance ministry and industry demands is enabled by the following:

A) By fulfilling the following prescriptions from my research in Table 14
B) By having a **control plan** to sustain these steps and for accountability and adjustment when progress is off target

Table 14: Best Practices for Balancing Ministry in the Industry	Examples
1 – Demonstrate your mission for the greater good and growth of the kingdom. Demonstrate your conviction for ministry through your spiritual gifting, testimony, charitable cause, or other commission for humanity for training and developing others in ministry to sustain the kingdom. Reference scriptures: James 2:14–17 Matthew 6:33 Matthew 25:35	Lacrae's Reach Life Ministries: "We want to use the platform we've been given by God to spark a movement of believers that are committed to seeing the gospel saturated in all areas of their life. We are a ministry in its infancy with a commitment to bridging the gap between biblical truth and the urban context."[1] Mahalia Jackson and The Staple Singers used their celebrity to aid in the civil rights movement. Thomas Dorsey started NCGCC; James Cleveland launched GMWA; Edwin and Walter Hawkins launched their Worship and Arts Seminar; Donnie McClurkin hosted a very affordable and informative Perfecting Ministries Conference. Budget time and expense for legitimate charitable/non-profitable causes, give concerts that transform lives, assist with disaster relief, or meet other humanitarian needs. Artists United For Haiti (K. Franklin). Participate in opportunities at your local church or your local community if you do not have your own separate mission. It can be formal or informal until you become established enough to manage it in a more structured manner. The Gospel Music One Sound Project was for this research but can be leveraged as an ongoing mission for sowing back into developing others for music ministry in the church, community, and industry. The event was funded by donations and personal finances. A cause attached to the event was to collect funds and send a portion of proceeds to the Salvation Army for the East Coast Floods Effort for the people of South Carolina. As a result, $500 was donated for this special cause. – A. Arnold-McFarland

---

[1] *ReachLife Ministries*: https://www.mightycause.com/organization/Reachlife-Ministries

Table 14: Best Practices for Balancing Ministry in the Industry	Examples
2 – Focus on winning souls instead of on winning sales (K. Franklin). Your platform for music is a method for evangelism in church and non-church venues. Your lifestyle should serve as a role model to win souls, encourage salvation, and encourage the saints. Reference scriptures: Luke 14:23 Matthew 9:37–38 Matthew 28:18–20 Romans 10:11–15 Philemon 6 Colossians 3:23 Proverbs 16:3	Lecrae offers prayer meetings before NBA games. Kirk Franklin shares his testimony to help others transform their lives, and he has helped bridge sacred and secular artists for ministry purposes. Do not be afraid to cross over into culturally different opportunities. Andraé Crouch, Israel Houghton, BeBe and CeCe Winans, Lecrae, Yolanda Adams, and Mary Mary are just a few artists who have cross-cultural and cross-genre appeal. Roberta Thorpe played gospel music at the Cotton Club to take her music to those who may not attend church. In the 1980s, contemporary group Commissioned provided an altar call in their concerts offering Christ to those who attended.
3 – Be accessible and approachable. Stay abreast of practices and technology standards in the industry to make your music ministry accessible and approachable. This also sustains exposure and keeps a pulse on the spiritual needs of people. Reference scriptures: Exodus 31:1–5 Titus 1:7 2 Timothy 3:17	Numerous gospel artists are now on Periscope, a new social media tool that allows real-time tweets and response to followers. Artists are involved in reality TV, have roles as radio personalities, and participate in workshops and seminars for face time with their followers.

Table 14: Best Practices for Balancing Ministry in the Industry	Examples
4 – Learn the business and stay relevant. Acquire knowledge on your own initiative of all aspects of the business of the music industry (copyrights, radio, publishing, recording, contracts, accounting, legalities, artist development, distribution, and promotions). Also study the specifics of the gospel music industry so it can be effectively leveraged as a platform for ministry. Operate your pursuits as a legal business with a trade name and have strategic planning sessions to grow it. Always maintain your integrity. Scripture references: 2 Timothy 2:15 2 Corinthians 9:6–7 Luke 16:11 Luke 14:28 Habakkuk 2:2–3	Increase business acumen with regular and frequent study of trade websites, magazines, and events like the Gospel Music Industry Round Up, Billboard Charts, SAGMA (the Stellar Awards), The Grammy Awards, and musicbizacademy.com. Attend conferences and seminars that provide face time with industry professionals. Understand the legal risks. Join professional organizations (BMI, ASCAP, SESAC) for song protection and to stay informed. See Table 13 as an example of information obtained from Donnie McClurkin's Perfecting Music Conference.

Table 14: Best Practices for Balancing Ministry in the Industry	Examples
5 – Present an art form with sincerity. "It should reflect where we are and our personal spiritual growth with God. If that's not our top priority, then our art form is going to be very shallow. It should not be for the sole purpose of the art form itself. If it's that, we'll suffer. We have to make sure people can feel the sincerity of our own testimony and our own journey so they know this is something that is really real for us."[2] – K. Franklin Scripture references: Colossians 3:16 Titus 2:7 Psalm 108:1 John 4:23–24	Thomas Dorsey wrote his most famed composition, "Precious Lord, Take My Hand," out of pain during the lowest point in his life in 1932 upon the news of the death of his wife and child in childbirth. This song became a hymn standard and favorite of Martin Luther King, who requested hearing it sung by Mahalia Jackson. She sang it at his funeral in 1968. Aretha Franklin sang it at Mahalia's funeral in 1972. Leontyne Price sang it at Lyndon B. Johnson's funeral in 1973. It has been recorded by Elvis Presley, Al Greene, Ike and Tina Turner, Andraé Crouch, Pat Boone, BB King, Beyoncé, Merle Haggard, and Ledisi, among other notable recordings.

---

[2] "Take My Hand, Precious Lord." *Wikipedia: https://en.wikipedia.org/wiki/Take_My_Hand,_Precious_Lord.*

Table 14: Best Practices for Balancing Ministry in the Industry	Examples
6- Maintain your relationship with God through regular study, practice, and accountability of your Christian faith. Practice your ministry in the local church or community and make time to be ministered to. Balance time between church obligations and your gospel artist pursuits, being careful not to overcommit. Spiritual wellness is a must for ministry and the industry. Spiritual discernment is needed for decisions with sound judgment. It also helps you maintain accountability and humility. Too many musicians get lost to the wayside spiritually because they are so busy working in ministry and not growing from ministry. It is important that your musical message remains biblically sound and theologically accurate. You are accountable for the message you send. Singing or playing for the church or the industry does not guarantee entry to the kingdom. Scripture references: Romans 12:2 Jeremiah 29:11 Revelation 3:20 John 14:6	At the Donnie McClurkin's Perfecting Music Conference in 2011, Israel Houghton talked about how singing is a part of one's worship life: "Sunday is usually the only time we see worship happening. The way we conduct our lives and the way we interact with people is an act of worship. Heart placement is vital to effective worship. He feels compelled to change the perception of many musicians in today's church settings. Musicians can change this perception by focusing on gratitude, generosity, grace and godliness." At the same conference William Becton stated, "Music ministry leadership must set a standard of sanctification for others to follow and should resist the flesh and carnality, as did the Levites. The scriptural reference for this discussion was 1 Corinthians 1:10, where the apostles teach that as Christians we are to speak the same things and be of the same mind and same judgment without division. This is the expectation for all ministry leadership, including music, as it relates to the vision of the pastor."

Table 14: Best Practices for Balancing Ministry in the Industry	Examples
7- Maintain a good reputation and good relationships with genuine people who can mentor you and whom you can influence. Stay connected with and honor your predecessors. Stay connected with the next generation of artists on the gospel music continuum, who will stand on your shoulders. Establish and sustain genuine relationships with industry professionals who can mentor your journey. Keep a good reputation in ministry and industry. This grants favor, and favor is better than riches. Network with, support, and celebrate others. Scripture references: Romans 15:5–6 Galatians 6:2 Proverbs 22:1	Entry into the gospel music industry is proven based on skill and relationships. Master your gift and take critiques. Dorsey, Cleveland, and Franklin are key examples of artists who made opportunities accessible for others. Established artists mentor and develop up-and-coming artists. Also, share your knowledge with those who will come after you. This helps you stay sharp in your own abilities and keeps you relevant with upcoming generations.

Implications

From a theological perspective, the gospel artist is uniquely positioned to use the national stage of the gospel music industry to make an impact that transforms the lives of people and restores hope in Christianity. We live in an era of mass shootings, religious persecution against Christians, continued social injustice of police brutality, and black-on-black crime. These news flashes are depressive and oppressive. Christianity is a religion that seeks to fulfill promises to the socially oppressed. Music has always accompanied major social movements of African-Americans, and now is the time to leverage our gifts to propel us forward. The gospel artist can use music to evangelize and reach people who are losing hope in true Christianity. It is time to use the national platform and creatively reach weary and hopeless non-believers and to encourage believers. The direction in which African-American worship is evolving seems bleak as we continue to see behavior and discernment demonstrated among Christians that do not align with Scripture, godly living, and Christian teaching. This indicates that there is a lack of understanding or lack of desire to worship God in spirit and in truth. Thus, we see a lack of spiritual skill set to evolve worship that nurtures spiritual growth toward transformed lives. The coming of this time is foretold in the scripture below. Therefore, we must use our artistic abilities to regain a strong faith as a pillar in the community, taking our music to minister to the oppressed and faithless, wherever they are, without concern of controversy.

> For the time will come when they will not endure sound doctrine, but according to their own desires, because they have itching ears, they will heap up for themselves teachers; and they will turn their ears away from the truth, and be turned aside to fables. But you be watchful in all things, endure afflictions, do the work of an evangelist, fulfill your ministry.
> – 2 Timothy 4:3–5

As the historical development indicated in the analysis, controversy has always followed the continuum of gospel music. Gospel music by definition has been the lyrical spiritual outcry of the "common" people who experience the realities of life arranged to music influenced by the popular culture. The drivers of change on the gospel music continuum have been the young adults or voices engaged with civic activity of the social situation. Controversy has been a leading indicator in gospel music of upcoming social acceptance of evolutions in art form, practices, and venue. The next generation or upcoming artists benefit from the struggle and rejection of their predecessor.

History indicates a "major change" approximately every 30 to 35 years in gospel music resulting along the continuum and amidst the controversy. This was incubated with the Fisk Jubilee Singers in the late 1870s to just before 1900, approximately 30 years later, when gospel music was birthed and revolutionized with the aid of Thomas Dorsey. In the middle of the golden age, approximately 1965, James Cleveland was the king of gospel, mass producing groups and choirs. Shortly after, in 1970, Edwin Hawkins and Andraé Crouch birthed the contemporary sound. In the mid-1990s, Kirk Franklin burst on the scene with an urban appeal and took the baton into the new millennium. He revolutionized gospel music in quality on all levels, brought in numerous new artists, and became an entrepreneur in his role as a music industry professional. He mastered the effectiveness of collaboration and demonstrated a heart for humanity in his spiritual message. In approximately 2025 to 2030, we can anticipate a new wave of change in gospel music to take it to the next level.

One might think that over the 85-year life span of gospel music, the extremes of the continuum, the developmental and traditional era of Dorsey (1920–1930s), and the contemporary millennium era of Franklin (2000–present) would be quite different. As revolutionaries of their eras, they both had similar concepts in practices, as compiled in Table 15 at the end of this section. We may see these same concepts unfold in our next drum major of gospel. Kirk Franklin's intro lines, "Has gospel music gone too far?" asked at the beginning of his controversial hit "Stomp," sent a buzz of surprise to the secular music world and some rejection to the sacred music platforms. When we hear it now, it seems traditional compared with where gospel music has gone. Now, 20 years later, as Franklin has grown spiritually and even more creatively, he has taken gospel music even further, perhaps with not as much controversy.

Through it all, one foundational element of the African-American worship experience that has transcended the stylistic adaptations they represent and those in between is Ntu. These practitioners, like James Cleveland, Shirley Caesar, and many other famed exalters on the continuum, know how to make room for the spirit to move. Even an average singing Spirit-led voice like that of Thomas Dorsey or Kirk Franklin, who do not proclaim to singers, can carry a tune that will spread from heart to heart. The Spirit can move when a sincere heart lifts sincere lyrics, regardless of the era.

This is that spiritual encounter that happens when the anointing "stops by" as a message is sincerely preached and delivered in the unique "hoop" or rhythmic delivery of the black preacher, and the people are responsive to the presence of the Lord. The music is hummed or played between the breaths of the exalter. This experience, often called "having church," is what the African-American worshiper seeks and has connected with since being enslaved from West Africa. This experience soothes the heart and lifts burdens for the oppressed and weary. It celebrates triumphs and encourages through trials. A song of sincerity can be lifted, and everyone follows the move of the Spirit and joins in. This was demonstrated when President Obama had the difficult task at historic Emmanuel AME of delivering the eulogy of Rev. Clementa Pickney and commemorating all the Charleston 9. At the climax of his message, he lifted the hymn "Amazing Grace," and the local congregation, as well as the nation watching it televised, joined in the singing. His message and song soothed the broken hearts of the families and consoled the nation through yet another tragedy that in a bittersweet way brought a victory over the controversial Confederate flag. Those who may have once been blind to the implications of the symbol could now see.

The early music of Africans in America, the folk style spirituals sung by slaves, ditties, and field hollers planted the seed for secular (blues/jazz/ragtime) and sacred (gospel) music in America. It has influenced other styles such as rock and roll, R&B, pop, and funk. Artists who participate on the national and global stage may step into the sacred space occasionally to share their spirituality.

Today gospel music, along with all these genres, has evolved and is very much a part of the fabric of the United States of America. Gospel music can be heard in the local church, the community, and the music industry across the board in nightclubs, at theme parks, on popular music soundtracks, and at the White House. I was reminded that the pain and oppression of our forefathers who lived the development of gospel music were not in vain when I saw the PBS Special *The Gospel Tradition: In Performance at the White House*. It was a part of an Emmy award nomination series called *In Performance at the White House* that has occurred for 37 years. This event honored gospel music and its profound influence on American music. It demonstrated how it has unified America across genres and racial and social divides. There was no more perfect host for this celebration than the first African-American president, Barak Obama, and First Lady Michelle Obama. The participants list was extensive, including Aretha Franklin, Bishop Rance Allen, Pastor Shirley Caesar, Tamela Mann, the Morgan State University Choir, and Michelle Williams.

Table 15: Commonalities	Thomas Dorsey	Kirk Franklin
Expanded venue.	Launched singing battles at high schools in Chicago.	Crossed over into the secular realm with airplay and performances in secular venues.
Developed a process for developing others.	NCGCC (Dorsey Convention).	Sunday Best.
Influenced careers of numerous others or collaborated with others.	Roberta Martin, Mahalia Jackson, Willie Mae Ford. Collaborated with Sallie Martin.	Tamela Mann, Myron Butler, Isaac Caree. Collaborative work includes "Lean on Me," "Stomp," Artists United for Haiti.
Demonstrated creative and sincere penmanship for timeless art that continues to touch souls today.	Wrote over 1,000 songs. Famed for "Precious Lord, Take My Hand."	Extensive discography of over 14 albums, not including songs written and produced for others. Example hit is "The Reason Why We Sing."
Merged popular music with spiritual lyrics for a stylist development.	Added blues and jazz progressions to evolve gospel hymns to a genre.	Added hip-hop flavor and R&B to develop urban contemporary.
Applied business savviness.	Charged for concerts, promoted sheet music, launched publishing company, leveraged promotions and exposure practices from blues arena.	Launched multiple streams of income (producing music, live performance House of Blues, radio station, writing books, movies, television shows).

Recommendations for Continued Study

This study looked at the evolution of the African-American worship experience from the perspective of the independent gospel artist. The primary focus was on the gospel music industry, yet it took into consideration the local church and the community since these two venues interact with the gospel music industry. There are several opportunities to replicate the process for continued study.

As Pastor William Becton discussed during the Gospel Music One Sound Project Day 1 Seminar, the gospel music industry influences what happens in local church and community music ministries. He alluded to the thought that more churches should take the opportunity to partner with their local worship leaders/artists to write music out of the church and influence the industry. His concern is that not all music that gets exposure on the radio is the best music theologically to influence the church. There is an opportunity to take this angle and look at solutions for the church to have a bigger role in influencing the industry with music that speaks prophetically to what the move of God is for the spiritual era.

Additionally, there is the opportunity to continue Gospel Music One Sound as an ongoing community of practice for practitioners of gospel music in the three main venues: church, community, and industry. It would be interesting to follow a sample group of gospel artists and church ministries that utilized the SWOT analysis and applied the practical applications and best practices discussed as improvements for the next year. An evaluation to measure current progress of the prescriptions could serve as a baseline. Goals in each area could be set, along with a timeline for reaching them. At milestones and the end of the timeline, the current state would be compared with the future state. For example, I now have more insight to apply to my strategies and plans for my ensemble Blessed Union, The Group. We can build on the SWOT analysis and define a timeline for applying the prescriptions.

A third area for recommended study is to adapt this study by looking at how worship arts, not just gospel music, have evolved as an entity in the African-American worship experience and how they can be used more creatively for improved effectiveness of the experience. The Gospel Music One Sound Concert was a contemporary concept in a normally traditional worship space at Oak City Baptist Church. It used acting, praise dancing, teaching, live music, lighting, audio, and projection screens interactively as a learning and worship experience. This approach moved people out of their comfort zones and created new possibilities for this worship space. Positive feedback was received on the information people learned from the onsite activities as well as the online activities.

CONCLUSION

In conclusion, this work has provided me with a tremendous opportunity to take a deep dive into a passion I have had for as long as I can remember. I have had inquiries from individuals with interest in attending the same institution. They thought this degree was a standard curriculum. I explained that it was a hybrid approach at the Graduate Theological Foundation in the Creative Arts Doctor of Ministry Degree. Perhaps there is an opportunity to offer a curriculum specific to African-American worship. I am excited about the possibilities this endeavor will afford me as a scholar, professional consultant, and practitioner of gospel music. I look forward to continued study and what God has in store for me next in this arena.

BIBLIOGRAPHY

Primary Sources

Abbington, James (2001). *Readings in African-American Church Music and Worship.* Chicago: GIA Publications, Inc.

Boyer, Horace C. (1995). *The Golden Age of Gospel.* Montgomery, Ala.: Black Belt Press.

Burnim, V. B., and Portia K Maultsby (2005). *African-American Music: An Introduction.* New York: Routledge.

Cone, James A. (1991). *The Spirituals and the Blues: An Interpretation.* Ossining, N.Y.: Orbis Books.

Costen, Melva (1993). *African-American Christian Worship.* Nashville: Abingdon Press.

Davis, L. Stanley (speaker) (2015). *Chicago: Roots in Gospel Music Webinar.* Personal communication retrieved Nov. 10, 2015.

GIA Publications, Inc. (2001). *African-American Heritage Hymnal.* Chicago: GIA Publications, Inc.

Heilbut, Anthony (1997). *The Gospel Sound: Good News and Bad Times. 25th Anniversary Edition.* New York: Proscenium Publishers, Inc.

Hayes, Diana (2002). *Forged in the Fiery Furnace.* Ossining, N.Y.: Orbis Books.

Lincoln, C. Eric, and Lawrence H. Mamiya (1990). *The Black Church in the African-American Experience.* Durham, N.C.: Duke University Press.

Marovich, Bob (2015). *Interview: Gospel Music Milestones 2000–2015.* Oct 21, 2015.

Reagon, Bernice J. (1992). *We'll Understand It Better By and By.* Washington, DC: Smithsonian Institution Press.

Southern, Eileen (1997). *The Music of Black Americans: A History* (3rd ed). New York: W. W. Norton and Company.

Thurman, Howard (1975). *Deep River and The Negro Spiritual Speaks of Life and Death.* Richmond, Va.: Friends Press.

Turner, Steve (2010). *An Illustrated History of Gospel Music.* Oxford, Eng.: Lion Hudson PLC

Wise, Raymond (2002). *Defining African-American Gospel Music by Tracing Its Historical and Musical Development from 1900 to 2000.*(Electronic dissertation). Retrieved from https://etd.ohiolink.edu/. (Document number osu1243519734).

Secondary Sources

Adams, Yolanda (2015). About Yolanda. Retrieved Dec .2, 2015, from http://yolandaadamslive.com/v2/about/.

All Music (2015). *Commissioned.* Retrieved Oct. 7, 2015, from http://www.All Music.com/artist/commissioned-mn0000094658/discography.

All Music (2015). *Israel Houghton.* Retrieved Oct. 7, 2015, from http://www.allmusic.com/artist/israel-houghton-mn0000776576.

All Music (2015). *Kirk Franklin.* Retrieved Oct. 7, 2015, from http://www.allmusic.com/artist/kirk-franklin-mn0000083095.

All Music (2015). *Lecrae.* Retrieved Oct. 7, 2015, from http://www.allmusic.com/artist/lecrae-mn0000403784.

All Music (2015). *Mary Mary.* Retrieved Oct. 7, 2015, from http://www.allmusic.com/artist/mary-mary-mn0000860985.

All Music (2015). *Staple Singers.* Retrieved Oct. 7, 2015, from http://www.All Music.com/artist/the-staple-singers-mn0000577235/biography.

All Music (2015). *William Becton.* Retrieved Oct. 7, 2015, from http://www.allmusic.com/artist/william-becton-mn0000682321.

All Music (2015). *Yolanda Adams.* Retrieved Oct. 7, 2015, from http://www.allmusic.com/artist/yolanda-adams-mn0000690718.

All Music (2015). *The Winans.* Retrieved Oct. 7, 2015, from http://www.All Music.com/artist/the-winans-mn0000576839/discography.

Becton (2015). Gospel Music One Sound Project. Personal communication. Retrieved Nov, 20–21, 2015.

Best, H. (2003). *Unceasing Worship: A Biblical Perspective on Worship and the Arts.* Downers Grove, Ill.: Intervarsity Press.

BET (2015). *The Bobby Jones Show.* Retrieved Oct. 5, 2015, from http://www.bet.com/shows/bobby-jones-gospel.html.

Black Gospel (2015). *BeBe and CeCe Winans, Mary Mart to Be Honored at the 2016 Trailblazers Awards in Atlanta.* http://blackgospel.com/?s=BeBe+and+CeCe#.VmfGh03ltcs.

California Worship Center (2015). *About Us.* Retrieved Dec. 1, 2015, from http://californiaworshipcenter.com/.

Carpenter, Bil (2005). *Uncloudy Days: The Gospel Music Encyclopedia.* San Francisco: Backbeat Books.

Castellini, Michael (2013). *Sit In, Stand Up and Sing Out! Black Gospel Music and the Civil Rights Movement.* Thesis, Georgia State University.

Chenu, Bruno (2003). *The Trouble I've Seen. The Big Book of Negro Spirituals.* Valley Forge, Pa.: Judson Press.

Collins, Lisa (2015). *The Gospel Music Industry Round Up.* Los Angeles: Eye on Gospel Publications.

Daniels, Antonio Maurice (2012). *Bridging the Gap Between Sacred and Secular.* http://soultrain.com/2012/11/16/bridging-the-gap-between-sacred-and-secular-kirk-franklins-prominence/.

Gospel Music (n.d.). Dictionary. Retrieved July 2, 2015, from http://dictionary.reference.com/browse/gospel-music.

Fisk Jubilee Singers (2015). *About Us.* Retrieved Oct. 5, 2015, from http://www.fiskjubileesingers.org/about.html.

Ford, S. (2009). *Is Your Music Department Ministry or Misery?* Middletown, Del.: S. Ford Music Publishing.

Harris, Michael W. (1992). *The Rise of Gospel Blues. The Music of Thomas Andrew Dorsey in the Urban Church.* New York: Oxford University Press.

Hawkins Gospel Conference (2015). *About Edward and Walter Hawkins Music and Arts Love Fellowship Conference.* Retrieved Oct. 5, 2015, from http://hawkinsgospelconference.org/.

I Six Sigma (2015). What Is Six Sigma? Retrieved Dec. 10, 2015, from http://www.isixsigma.com/dictionary/six-sigma.

Johnson, Birgitta (2008). *"O for A Thousand Songs to Sing." Music and Worship in African-American Megachurches in Los Angeles.* (Electronic dissertation). Retrieved from books.google.com. (Document number UMI 3322020).

Jones, Arthur C. (2005). *Wade in the Water: The Wisdom of the Spirituals.* Boulder, Colo.: Leave a Little Room Publishing.

Kenon, M., and Damon Stout (producers and directors) (2004). *Higher Ground: Voices of Contemporary Gospel Music* [DVD] United States. (Available from Image Entertainment Inc., 9333 Oso Avenue, Chatsworth, CA 91311) .

King, Darrell (2010). *This Business of Gospel Music.* N.p.: Gospel Knowledge Books.

Kirk Franklin (2015). Album. Retrieved Dec. 1, 2015. from http://www.kirkfranklin.com/.

Lecrae (2015). About. Retrieved Dec. 1, 2015. from http://www.lecrae.com/.

Lewis, Charles E. (2011). *Reconciliation of Worship in the Black Church: Spontaneous Worship.* Bloomington, Ind.: iUniverse.

Lowe, Valerie G. (2003). "The Rebirth of Kirk Franklin," *Charisma.* Retrieved Nov. 30, 2015, from http://www.charismamag.com/site-archives/146-covers/cover-story/831-the-rebirth-of-kirk-franklin.

Mary Mary (2013). *I Love Mary Mary, About.* Retrieved Dec. 1, 2013, from http://ilovemarymary.com/about/.

Nielsen (2014). *Music album sales in the United States from 2008 to 2014, by genre (in millions).* Retrieved May 16, 2015, from http://www.statista.com/statistics/188910/us-music-album-sales-by-genre-2010/.

Negro Spirituals (2015). *History.* Retrieved Oct. 2, 2015, from http://www.negrospirituals.com/history.htm.

PBS (2004). *The Slave Experience: Education, Arts and Culture.* Retrieved Dec. 2, 2015, from http://www.pbs.org/wnet/slavery/experience/education/history.html.

PBS (2015). *The Gospel Tradition: In performance at the White House.* Retrieved Dec. 10, 2015, from http://www.pbs.org/inperformanceatthewhitehouse/shows/gospel-tradition/

Rowen, Beth, and Borgna Brunner (2015). *Great Days in Harlem.* Retrieved Oct. 2, 2015, from http://www.infoplease.com/spot/bhmharlem1.html.

Smithsonian Institution (2015). *Martin and Morris Music Company.* Retrieved Oct. 3, 2015, from http://historywired.si.edu/detail.cfm?ID=279.

Salzman, Jack (1993). *The African-American Experience.* New York: McMillian Library Reference USA.

Spencer, Jon Michael (1992). *Black Hymnody: A Hymnological History of the African-American Church.* Knoxville, Tenn.: University of Tennesee Press.

------ (1990). *Protest and Praise.* Minneapolis: Augsburg Fortress.

Tanner, Michael (2015). *The Gospel According to Brother Michael: A Brief History of Anthem, Spiritual, and Gospel Music from Early Slavery to the Mid Twentieth Century.* Retrieved Oct. 2, 2015, from http://www.kusp.org/playlists/crosscurrents/history.html.

USC Digital Library (2015). *Gospel Music History Archive.* Retrieved Oct. 2, 2015, from http://digitallibrary.usc.edu/cdm/timeline/collection/p15799coll9.

Walker, James A. (2010). *The Business of Urban Music: A Practical Guide to Achieving Success in the Industry, from Gospel to Funk to R&B to Hip-Hop.* New York: Billboard Books.

Walker, Wyatt Tee (1979). *Somebody's Calling My Name: Black Sacred Music and Social Change.* Valley Forge, Pa.: Judson Press.

William Becton (2015). *Bio.* Retrieved Dec. 2, 2015, from http://williambecton.org/.

Gospel Music Industry Professional Events

Gospel Music Workshop of America (GMWA)

Harley, Sanchez (2012). Personal communication. *GMWA Conference course. The Business of Gospel Music.* Retrieved July 12, 2012.

Hillsman, Joan (2012). Personal communication. *GMWA Conference course Research Methods.* Retrieved July 9–12, 2012.

Johnson, Garrett (2012). Personal communication. *GMWA Conference course. The Business of Gospel Music.* Retrieved July 9–12, 2012.

Joseph, Clark (2012). Course material. *GMWA Conference course. Gospel Chords.* Retrieved July 9–12, 2012.

Pernell, Franklin (2012). Personal communication. *GMWA Conference course. The Business of Gospel Music.* Retrieved July 11, 2012.

Reed, Shirley. (2012) Course material. Personal communication. *GMWA Conference course. The Theory and Theology of Praise and Worship.* Retrieved July 9–12, 2012.

Perfecting Music Conference

Butler, Myron, Kerry Douglas, and Aaron Lindsay (2011). Personal communication. *Perfecting Music Conference: Recording 101.* Retrieved April 29–30, 2011.

Douglas, Kerry, and Aaron Lindsay (2011). Personal communication. *Perfecting Music Conference: Real Deal Points.* Retrieved April 29–30, 2011.

Douglas, Kerry, Melanie Clark, and Gary Tom (2011). Personal communication. *Perfecting Music Conference: Commercial Radio.* Retrieved April 29–30, 2011.

Douglas, Kerry, Melanie Clark, Israel Houghton, and Aaron Lindsay (2011). Personal communication. *Perfecting Music Conference: Starting a Record Label.* Retrieved April 29–30, 2011.

Douglas, Kerry (2011). Personal communication. *Perfecting Music Conference: Marketing and Branding.* Retrieved April 29–30, 2011.

Houghton, Israel (2011). Personal communication. *Perfecting Music Conference: Praise and Worship.* Retrieved April 29–30, 2011.

McClurkin, Donnie, and William Becton (2011). Personal communication. *Perfecting Music Conference: The Arts, Music and The Pastor.* Retrieved April 29–30, 2011.

McClurkin, Donnie (2011). Personal communication. *Perfecting Music Conference: Evangelism.* Retrieved April 29–30, 2011.

Morgan, Wes (2011). Personal communication. *Perfecting Music Conference: The Ministry of Wes Morgan.* Retrieved April 29–30, 2011.

The Stellar Awards Gospel Music Academy / The Stellar Awards

Cole, Dennis (2013). Personal communication via email and phone interview. *SAGMA and The Stellar Awards.* Retrieved April 1–26, 2013.

Davis, L. Stanley (2013). Personal communication via live interview. *SAGMA and The Stellar Awards.* Retrieved January 19, 2013.

Divine, Dana (2013). Personal communication via live interview. *SAGMA and The Stellar Awards.* Retrieved January 19, 2013.

Faine, Leanne (2013). Personal communication via live interview. *SAGMA and The Stellar Awards.* Retrieved January 18, 2013.

Jackson, Don (2013). Personal communication via email. *SAGMA and The Stellar Awards.* Retrieved April 23, 2013.

African-American Church Music Series

Abbington, Dr. James (2011). Personal communication. *African-American Church Music Series.* Retrieved August 27, 2011.

Homiletics, Hymns, and Spirituals Conference

Abbington, Dr. James (2011). Personal communication. *Homiletics, Hymns, and Spirituals Conference.* Retrieved February 18, 2012.

Powery, Dr. Luke (2012). Personal communication. *Homiletics, Hymns, and Spirituals Conference.* Retrieved February 17, 2012.

LIST OF TABLES, FIGURES, AND IMAGES

See Image 8 in Appendix 1 for the historical time frames discussed prior to the era of traditional gospel music.

Identification	Description	Page Number
Figure 1	Continuum of Black Sacred Music (Pre-Gospel Era)	119
Table 1-A	The Pre-Gospel Era (1619–1865 to Early 1900s) Black Sacred Music Social Acceptance vs. Evolution of Black Sacred Music	120
Table 1-B	The Pre-Gospel Era (Prior to 1900) Influences on the Evolution of the Gospel Music Industry A Compilation of Contributions in Art Form, Practices (Industry/Ministry), and Venues	121
Table 1-C	The Pre-Gospel Era (1900–1920) Influences on the Evolution of the Gospel Music Industry A Compilation of Contributions in Art Form, Practices (Industry/Ministry), and Venues	123
Figure 2	Continuum of Gospel Music (Developmental and Traditional Gospel Era)	125
Table 2-A	Development (1920s–1930s) and Traditional Gospel Era (1930–1945) The Harlem Renaissance/New Negro Movement/Gospel Hymnody/Gospel Genre Gospel Music Social Acceptance vs. Evolution of Gospel Music	126
Table 2-B	Development (1920s–1930s) and Traditional Gospel Era (1930–1945) Influences on the Evolution of the Gospel Music Industry A Compilation of Contributions in Art Form, Practices (Industry/Ministry), and Venues	127
Figure 3	Continuum of Gospel Music (Golden Age / Modern Contemporary)	131

Identification	Description	Page Number
Table 3-A	Golden Age of Gospel Era (1945–1960s) (1960–1967 Modern Traditional Included) Gospel Music Social Acceptance vs. Evolution of Gospel Music	132
Table 3-B	Golden Age of Gospel Era (1945–1960s) (1960–1967 Modern Traditional Included) Influences on the Evolution of the Gospel Music Industry A Compilation of Contributions in Art Form, Practices (Industry/Ministry), and Venues	133
Figure 4	Continuum of Gospel Music (Modern Contemporary and New Millennium)	135
Table 4-A	Modern Contemporary (late 1960 –1970s)/(1980s–1990s) Gospel Music Social Acceptance vs. Evolution of Gospel Music	136
Table 4-B	Modern Contemporary (late 1960s–1970s)/(1980s–1990s) Influences on the Evolution of the Gospel Music Industry A Compilation of Contributions in Art Form, Practices (Industry/Ministry), and Venues	137
Table 5-A	Modern Contemporary, New Millennium (2000–2015) Gospel Music Social Acceptance vs. Evolution of Gospel Music	141
Table 5-B	Modern Contemporary Millennium (2000–2015) Influences on the Evolution of the Gospel Music Industry A Compilation of Contributions in Art Form, Practices (Industry/Ministry), and Venues	142
Table 6	Gospel Music One Sound Pre-Post Test Demographics	151
Table 7	Denominations	152
Table 8	Pre- and Post-Test Trend of Change	153
Table 9-A	SWOT Analysis: Blessed Union, The Group	154
Table 9-B	SWOT Matrix	155
Table 10	Quantitative Survey Results	156
Table 11 - A	Quantitative Pre- and Post-Test Survey Results	157
Table 11 - B	Quantitative Pre- and Post-Test Survey Results	157
Table 12 (Pre-Test)	Cross Tabulation: Styles of Gospel Music at Church vs Age Group of Participants	158

Identification	Description	Page Number
Table 13	Best Practices for Aspiring Gospel Artists, Perfecting Music Conference	159
Table 14	Best Practices for Balancing Ministry in the Industry	162
Table 15	Commonalities	169
Image 1	Gospel Music One Sound Project Facebook Flyer	182
Image 2	Facebook Group Screenshot	183
Image 3	Purpose Slide	184
Image 4	Three Venues for Worship Slide	185
Image 5	Sample Webinar Slide	185
Image 6	Gospel Music Definition Slide	186
Image 7	Mainline Churches of Today Slide	186
Image 8	Music of Mainline Churches Pre-Gospel Era Slide	187
Image 9	Gospel Music Evolution Eras Slide	187
Image 10	Subgenres of Modern Contemporary Slide	188
Image 11	Gospel Music Venues, Sample Artists Slide	188
Image 12	Effectiveness Today in Ministry and the Industry	189
Image 13	Qualities Demonstrated by an Effective Gospel Choir	189
Table 16	Compiled Qualitative Data	190
Image 14	Day 2 Concert—A Learning and Worship Experience	195
Table 17	African-American Spirituality Course	196

APPENDIX 1

Image 1

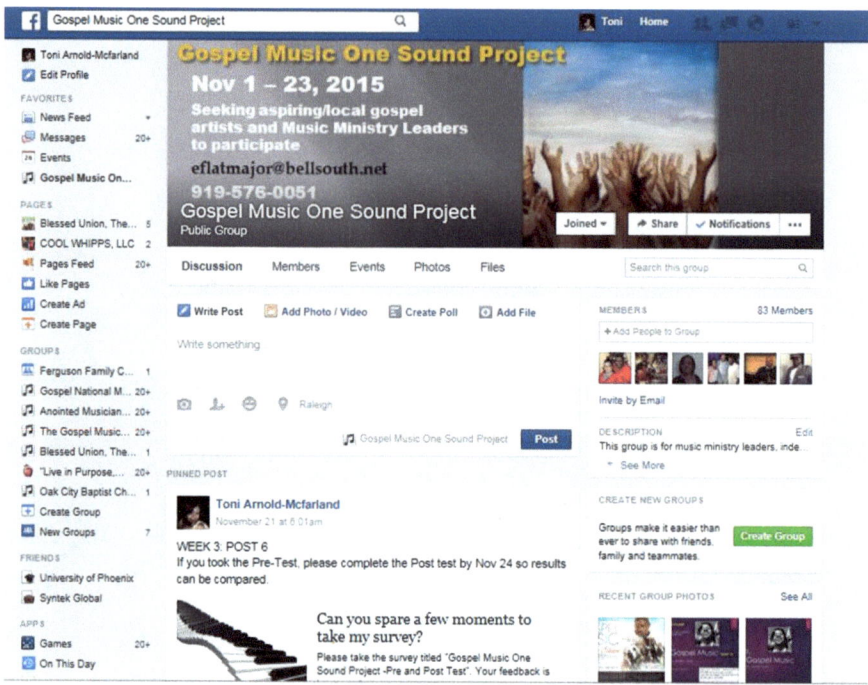

Image 2

This is a screen shot of the Facebook group used as a landing page for communication.

A truncated version of content presented during the Gospel Music One Sound Project is compiled below.

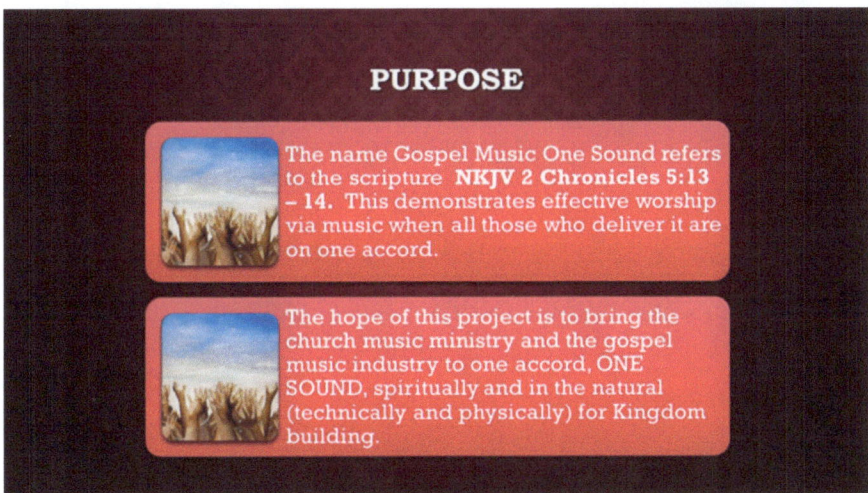

Image 3

Image 4

Image 5

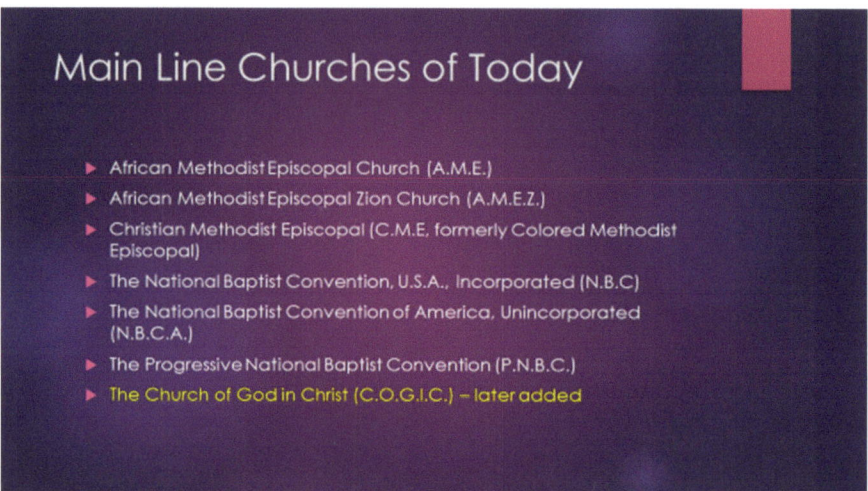

Image 6

Image 7

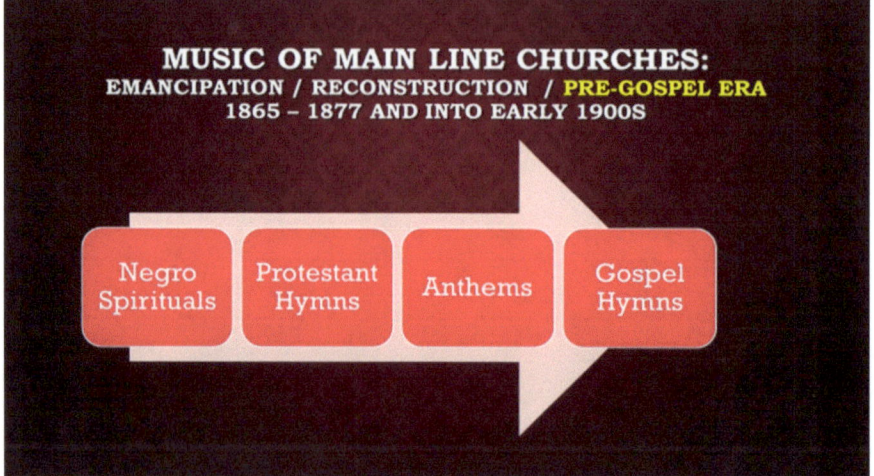

Image 8

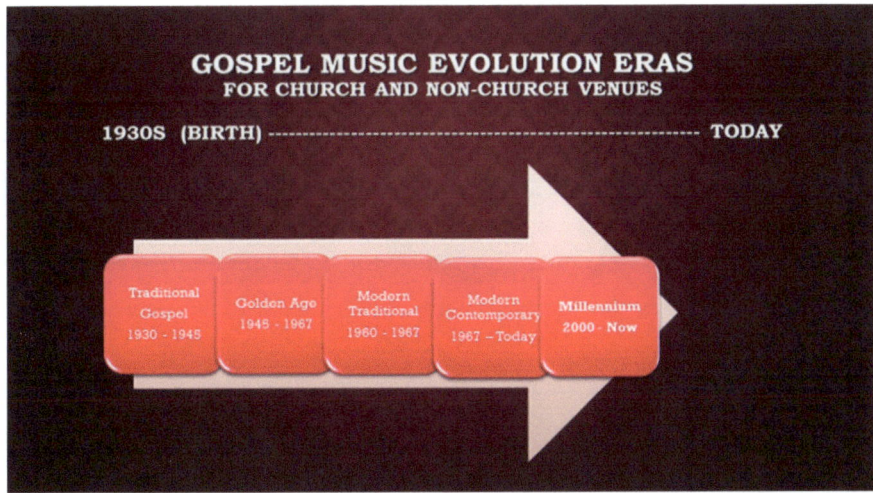

Image 9

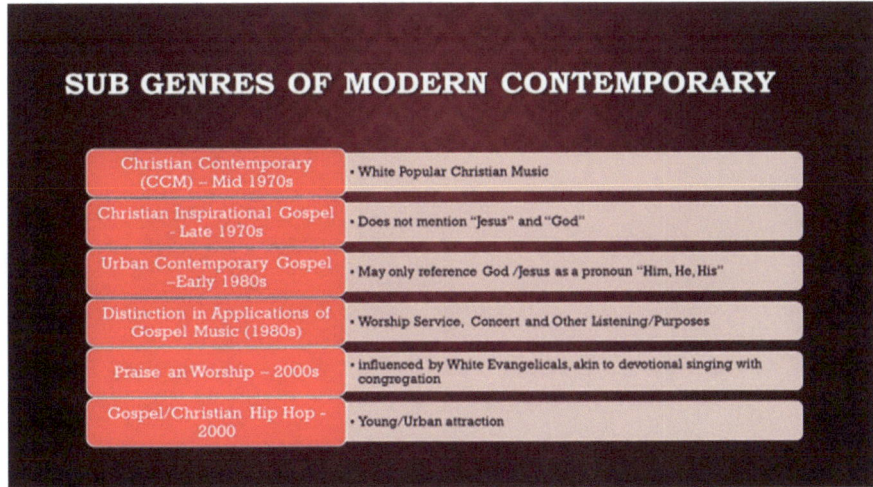

Image 10

Image 11

Practical Applications Quick Reference Guides

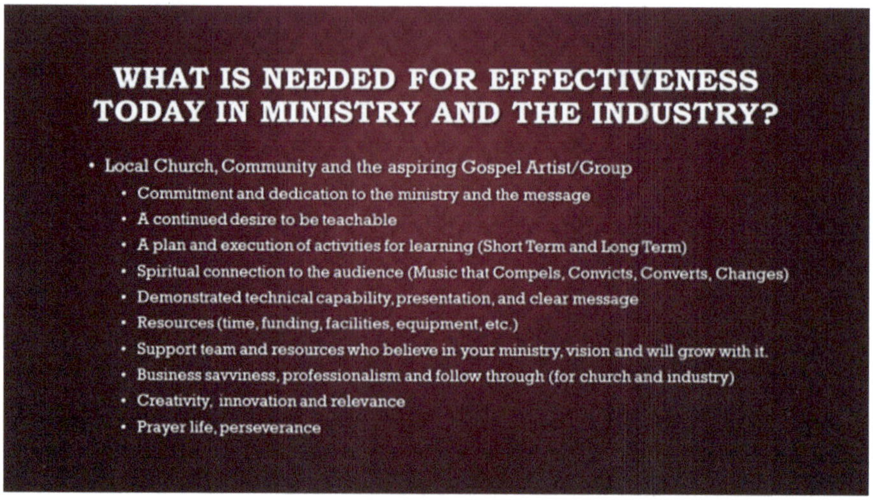

WHAT IS NEEDED FOR EFFECTIVENESS TODAY IN MINISTRY AND THE INDUSTRY?

- Local Church, Community and the aspiring Gospel Artist/Group
  - Commitment and dedication to the ministry and the message
  - A continued desire to be teachable
  - A plan and execution of activities for learning (Short Term and Long Term)
  - Spiritual connection to the audience (Music that Compels, Convicts, Converts, Changes)
  - Demonstrated technical capability, presentation, and clear message
  - Resources (time, funding, facilities, equipment, etc.)
  - Support team and resources who believe in your ministry, vision and will grow with it.
  - Business savviness, professionalism and follow through (for church and industry)
  - Creativity, innovation and relevance
  - Prayer life, perseverance

Image 12

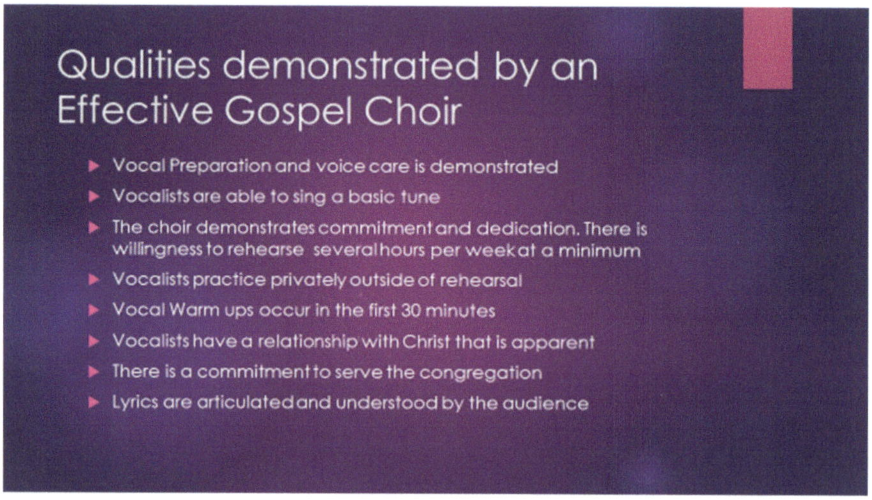

Qualities demonstrated by an Effective Gospel Choir

- Vocal Preparation and voice care is demonstrated
- Vocalists are able to sing a basic tune
- The choir demonstrates commitment and dedication. There is willingness to rehearse several hours per week at a minimum
- Vocalists practice privately outside of rehearsal
- Vocal Warm ups occur in the first 30 minutes
- Vocalists have a relationship with Christ that is apparent
- There is a commitment to serve the congregation
- Lyrics are articulated and understood by the audience

Image 13

Table 16: Compiled Qualitative Data

Questions/Top Issues from Surveys and Panel	Response (Based on Research)	Theme
- How do you generate change in the culture/traditions of the church choir? - When there is limited time for preparation (1–2 rehearsals per week), part-time staff, and increasing demands to improve and grow repertoire plus a lack of demonstrated interest from the singers to meet the demands, how do you move forward? - When you don't have that many members in the church, how do you establish an effective choir? - Why are churches slow in building their music department, budget, etc.? - What makes a music ministry effective? - How do you plan a vision for the music ministry? - To effectively manage the music department at a church, what steps must take place? *Top Issues from Surveys*: - Setting a budget that will retain the right skill sets for the music - Budget does not include additional seminars for choir members - A lack of awareness among leadership/pastors on relevant strategies for effective music ministry	These questions all stem from the lack of a strategic plan for operating or for growth. This conversation needs to align with the direction set for the music ministry and the church. Goals for effectiveness can be determined in the strategic discussion. The SWOT analysis can be used to set strategies. Small projects and initiatives may be birthed to resolve issues identified from the SWOT and the DMAIC methodology (Six Sigma) and can be used to improve processes. A music ministry strategist or consultant can help arrive at a plan for execution. Refer to Steven Ford's book *Is Your Music Department Ministry or Misery?* This is a practical guide for the pastor and music ministry leadership. Budgeting effectively is important to the growth of the church. Smaller churches generally lack knowledge about how to plan music and arts ministry. Creative options include using tracks or having times for congregational singing without instruments. There is a cost to doing ministry and clear responsibilities need to be defined for paid staff and for volunteers. Music seminars provide growth, relevancy, and continuous improvement. At a minimum, ongoing training should be required of the music ministry staff and officers. A starting budget can include sharing the cost of sending a few representatives to training. Then they can transfer the knowledge to others or co-host a small seminar in-house with another church.	Leadership/strategic planning and execution (short- and long-term goals).

Panel Questions/Top Issues from Surveys	Response (Based on Research)	Theme
How do we get members to fully participate in all aspects of music ministry? How can we be consistent? How can we build excitement in the choir when leadership has no excitement?	To get participation, have a music ministry "open house" or Sunday when interested parties can "try out" the choir before they commit. Attending a choir workshop or conference or hosting an event with outside participants can help build enthusiasm. Leadership can be involved in facilitating or speaking.	Commitment and engagement
How do we convince musicians how important it is for them to play their instruments at consistent sound levels in order to support the singers so the words being sung can be heard and understood at all times? How can we improve our quality of sound without paying an arm and a leg?	The audio and sound ministry needs trained technicians who can demonstrate their abilities. Choir members and musicians alike all need some level of audio and sound awareness. Find several churches about the same size as your church that have good sound and audio ministries. Ask them what they consider a reasonable budget for their growth. Plan to work toward a similar budget, adding equipment as funding allows.	Effectiveness of equipment—audio and sound
What do we do when we feel the choir has grown stagnant and is not growing spiritually? How do we handle friction, jealousy, and animosity among choir members?	Since choir today is volunteer in most churches and does not include demonstration of spiritual maturity, these issues exist. A good Bible study on the requirements of choir members technically and spiritually addresses immaturity. At a minimum, participants should be seeking salvation if they have not already professed it. Salvation can occur while being amidst believers through music or other means. Participants in all ministries, not just music, need to have consistent spiritual growth. Without this, there will always be carnal-minded conflicts. Refer to the preparation and training scriptures to bring more understanding and growth in what is modeled in the Bible for music ministry participation. Music ministry is not a place for people to be served; participants are called to be servants of the congregation. Refer also to Steve Ford's book mentioned in strategic planning on this chart.	Spiritual maturity

Panel Questions/Top Issues from Surveys	Response (Based on Research)	Theme
- Do you feel our praise team is as effective as it could be? If not, how can we make it better? - How do we teach the praise team to select appropriate songs for praise and worship? How do we get the choir to record their parts and study their music? - If a song is on the radio and the musician lowers the key, does this take away from the effectiveness of the song? - Do we have the right balance of focus between the quality vs. quantity of songs we perform? - How do we convince the music ministry the importance of teaching and learning songs well in advance so the singers can fully grasp them and deliver them with total freedom, confidence, and excellence? - Why do people feel all hymns are for old saints and not the younger generation? - How often should we conduct choir/music workshops? And what do we do when our musicians do not participate in the workshops?	All music ministry participants must be aware of the model for skill and delivery for singers and instrumentalist portrayed in Scripture. These can be used as a plan for protocol, roles, and responsibilities. Here are a few reference scriptures from Donnie McClurkin's Perfecting Music Conference: 1 Samuel 16:23; 1 Chronicles 15:22; 2 Chronicles 5:12–14; Psalm 100:1–2; Colossians 3:16. These are the goals for all the participants (singers, directors, worship leaders, instrumentalists). If they are not being held accountable and willing to submit to music ministry God's way, then we cannot expect the outcomes of excellence we desire. Spiritual commitment aligned with the preparation to invest in self and a teachable spirit create the ingredients for progress. Participants must be willing to respect correction, instructions, and decisions made that do not satisfy personal agendas and desires. The goal of every singer is to practice enough privately to be able to learn lyrics accurately, sing the part on pitch, and learn the arrangement of the song. The music director or minister of music should set basic technical requirements for participation. Some choir members may need to consider private lessons to meet these basic requirements. Use technology like smart phones to record rehearsals. The vocal parts can be recorded and placed on YouTube to provide a template for studying. If singers are not naturally musically inclined, practicing each phrase by repetition until it can be sung independently is the best method for retaining parts. If needed, have training to increase technology skill sets in the choir with devices and PCs to enable preparation outside of rehearsal.	Preparation, repertoire, training, and awareness

Panel Questions/Top Issues from Surveys	Response (Based on Research)	Theme
- How can we encourage choir members to rehearse outside of church? - What does private practice at home entail? *Top Issues from Survey:* - Exposing choir members to vocal development and seminars outside of rehearsal time. - Getting choir members to practice outside of rehearsal. - Choir members participating in various other ministries with overlapping commitments. - Consistency in choir member participation.	Choir members are usually involved in other ministries. Over-commitment will affect available time to prepare. They should take a good look at how many hours are needed for their personal lives and what they can commit to each ministry. This often affects consistency in participation. Lack of consistency hinders progress. An expectation needs to be set as a guideline. Quality of music prevails over quantity as the measure of success, although appropriate repertoire planning is important. This has to be balanced based on the time and capacity of the participants.	
- How do we effectively and without hurting feelings or self-esteem explain to a member of the music ministry that it may not be for him or her? - How do we handle the challenges of being placed as the minister of music after one was let go? - How do we handle our music ministry when the minister of music has lost his passion and doesn't want to learn anything new and doesn't want to resign?	First, music ministry participants must agree that leadership decisions are based on what is best for the overall progress of the music ministry. These decisions are not going to satisfy personal desires. It is helpful to have written guidelines and policies in place for requirements and expectations. Regular evaluation of performance is needed to progress in the work we do for ministry. When people do not progress and are provided time to improve and don't improve, then it is leadership's responsibility to manage issues, even with difficult conversations. This may include dismissing people from their season in a specific ministry. We are called to be good stewards for our contribution to ministry and have a role in accountability in how we oversee our area of ministry.	Personnel issues/ job fit, and performance

Panel Questions/Top Issues from Surveys	Response (Based on Research)	Theme
- How do we control strong personalities in the music ministry who have great demands without running them off? - Why are musicians not stable in churches? - Should choir participation, whether vocal or instrumental, be contingent on participation in other aspects of church life (such as Bible study, Sunday school, worship service) when they are not singing, playing, etc.?	Clarity on roles and responsibility will help as well. See scriptures in the preparation/training section. "Whatever you do, do it heartily, as to the Lord and not to men." – Colossians 3:23 NKJV "Since an overseer manages God's household, he must be blameless—not overbearing, not quick-tempered, not given to drunkenness, not violent, not pursuing dishonest gain." – Titus 1:7 NIV Backfilling a prior musician, choir/music director, or minister of music can be challenging if people are not open to change. This is a sign of stagnant spiritual growth. The new individual needs to be spiritually mature enough to set the standard and expectations to drive the transition. The pastor must be willing to support the change and cannot be influenced by choir members who circumvent the new leader and complain to the pastor. It is best if the pastor first speaks to the choir about his or her expectation of them to support the transition and points complainers back to the newly placed leadership before getting involved.	

Panel Questions/Top Issues from Surveys	Response (Based on Research)	Theme
- How do we control strong personalities in the music ministry who have great demands without running them off? - Why are musicians not stable in churches? - Should choir participation, whether vocal or instrumental, be contingent on participation in other aspects of church life (such as Bible study, Sunday school, worship service) when they are not singing, playing, etc.?	Clarity on roles and responsibility will help as well. See scriptures in the preparation/training section. "Whatever you do, do it heartily, as to the Lord and not to men." – Colossians 3:23 NKJV "Since an overseer manages God's household, he must be blameless—not overbearing, not quick-tempered, not given to drunkenness, not violent, not pursuing dishonest gain." – Titus 1:7 NIV Backfilling a prior musician, choir/music director, or minister of music can be challenging if people are not open to change. This is a sign of stagnant spiritual growth. The new individual needs to be spiritually mature enough to set the standard and expectations to drive the transition. The pastor must be willing to support the change and cannot be influenced by choir members who circumvent the new leader and complain to the pastor. It is best if the pastor first speaks to the choir about his or her expectation of them to support the transition and points complainers back to the newly placed leadership before getting involved.	

Day 2 Concert – A Learning and Worship Experience

Image 14

APPENDIX 2

Table 17: African-American Spirituality Course

Course Week	Key Learning Objectives	Key Take-Away Items	Relevance to Dissertation Thesis
Week 1 *Forged in the Fiery Furnace: African-American Spirituality*, by Diana Hayes *Introduction to Spirituality in African-American Context*	The first four chapters begin laying the foundation of understanding how African-American spirituality was forged in the fiery furnace of slavery. The author's approach to dissecting the content helps the reader understand African spirituality through the eyes of Western Christianity. Negro spirituals were birthed out of the slave experience. These so-called sorrow songs were ironically the quiet riot of slavery. They spoke messages that often deceived slave masters.	To understand African-American spirituality, one must first understand the ingredients that create the unique flavor of this ethnic group. What African-Americans have been taught about African religion has been influenced by European understanding of African religion. Spiritual remnants of our African origins and early beginnings are evident today in our culture.	*These points help display the evolution of gospel music.* Ironically, a system intended to enslave Africans living in a strange land births a strong faith that will become foundational in American history and in the fabric of American culture. Ntu is a key distinction in African-American worship today as spiritual encounters. It is the spiritual life force from our African origins that connects with ancestors and is incorporated into the Christianity of the slaves.

Course Week	Key Learning Objectives	Key Take-Away Items	Relevance to Dissertation Thesis
Week 2 *Emergence of the Black Church, Social Justice and Contemporary Witness* (Same book, chapters four through eight)	This is a review of the historical development of African-American spirituality from African spirituality. It reviews the Black Church, the primary denominations, and the various theologies that emerged. Chapter seven focuses on the spirituality of African-American women and our contributions to preserving our culture. Since slavery, African-American women have taken on the burdens of the world.	The author's underlying theme in these chapters conveys that African-Americans are not monolithic in our theologies; however, due to our common African roots, we are able to have unity in diversity. There is a spiritual connection among us that transcends denominations and even faiths. To soothe our souls, we find time to be artistic and creative with our hands, our minds, or in music or dance. We find quiet time in our faith. We are the first teachers of our children and others. We create our own welfare system.	Music speaks of and to the souls of African-Americans. Music of various genres has inspired movements of our people by empowering our social consciousness. African-American Christians have continued to hold strong and distinct traits of our spirituality. The result is the rationale for the cultural divide that exists every Sunday at 11:00 a.m. in America.
Week 3 *Deep River and the Negro Spiritual Speaks of Life and Death,* by Howard Thurman *Prayer and Mystical Experiences in the African-American Traditions*	Thurman dissects the lyrics of Negro spirituals in *Deep River* and interprets how they provide insight into life as a slave. He states that the Negro preacher was the greatest single factor in determining the spiritual destiny of the slave community. The articulation of the preacher's words gave slaves the endurance to live through struggles. The lyrics reference the Old and New Testaments, the world of nature, and the common-lot personal experiences of the slave, focusing on deliverance of the wrongfully oppressed.	Thurman's message set forth in the book is a message of hope in the struggle for courage, self-respect, and emotional security brought forth by his analysis and reflections of Negro spirituals.	***These points demonstrate the music and homiletics of the African-American church tradition.*** During slavery times and even in the civil rights movement, history demonstrates that the black preacher's role to relate and articulate to the current social state fueled the faith that brought about social change.

Course Week	Key Learning Objectives	Key Take-Away Items	Relevance to Dissertation Thesis
Week 4 *Deep River and the Negro Spiritual Speaks of Life and Death,* by Howard Thurman *Sacred Music and African-American Spirituality*	Negro spirituals are songs of protest and resistance. Thurman analyzes the lyrical content of various spirituals and notes themes and attitudes toward life and death. The second key theme on life reviewed is centered on a personal reaction to the vindictiveness and cruelty of one's fellows. It is noted that the slave master is not mentioned because he is seen as amoral.	Thurman notes that one attitude found in Negro spirituals is that some things in life are worse than death. Death is a private option and the attitude reflects thoughts of suicide or a death wish. A second attitude on death is one of resignation, mixed with fear and dread. Thurman explains that the slave's experience with death is immediate, inescapable, and dramatic. Thurman analyzes the attitude of life as a fact without reflection on the cause or reason. In general, life is viewed as an experience of evil, frustration, and despair. One mood focuses on the loneliness and discouragement of life.	*These points demonstrate the evolution of gospel music and the common theme of black sacred music.* My personal reflection is that we see the theme of personal commitment to life and in sojourning the pilgrimage in famous gospel lyrics like "I Don't Feel No Way Tired," "I'm on the Battlefield for My Lord," "I'm Still Holding On," and "I'll Go If I Have to Go by Myself," just to name a few. This theme is a constant in encouragement in sermons and songs in the Black Church.

Course Week	Key Learning Objectives	Key Take-Away Items	Relevance to Dissertation Thesis
Week 5 *The Spirituals and the Blues,* by James Cone *Interpreting Black Spirituals*	The primary theme of this text is that spirituals and the blues are about the power of song in the struggle for black survival. Week five provides Cone's interpretation of spirituals from the perspective of liberation theology. Throughout the text, he connects the lyrics of spirituals to black eschatology. This is from the viewpoint of the oppressed slave and reflects his or her thoughts on death, the final destiny, and the judgment of the oppressor—the slave owner. He speaks of how whites attempted to mentally enslave blacks by distorting the gospel to support their benefit as master and justification of enslavement. They tried to inflict mental servitude and acceptance of white values on the house slaves. Chapters four and five analyze how spirituals speak to faith and suffering in the Bible and black eschatology.	Musicologist William Francis Allen gave the creators of spirituals genius credit. However, he described slaves as half-barbarous and tried to assess the songs from the perspective of his own cultural experience. German musicologist Richard Walaschek denied the slaves the ability to produce the songs with originality and said the spirituals were imitations. Chapter three conveys the basic theological idea of the spirituals as this: God has not left the slaves alone and God will deliver them from human bondage.	*These points demonstrate the music of the African-American church tradition and the evolution of gospel music.* This diminishing of the spirituals and resistance to credit their creativity remind me of the initial response of white America to rap and hip-hop music. Black history is the record of the slave's resistance to human bondage, and in this case, against mental bondage.

Course Week	Key Learning Objectives	Key Take-Away Items	Relevance to Dissertation Thesis
Week 6 *The Spirituals and the Blues,* by James Cone *The Blues as Secular Spirituals*	The primary theme of this text is that spirituals and the blues are about the power of song in the struggle for black survival. Cone states that the blues depict the secular dimension of the black experience. Not all blacks were satisfied waiting on God to resolve black suffering. They chose non-spiritual responses to the day-to-day struggles of being black in America. Cone informs his audience that blues, like the spiritual, have African traits related to the functional character of West African music. The blues express conditions associated with the burden of freedom *after* the Civil War.	One must understand the culture and black experience of the slaves and post-slavery era to fully synthesize and interpret the blues. The primary similarity between spirituals and blues is that the seed of both expressions is trouble. In both styles, the singer must be old enough to have lived in disappointment and suffering. Cone explains that the blues imply a stubborn refusal to go beyond the existential problem and substitute other worldly answers. As a result, the blues ignore God by embracing the joys and sorrows of life. Spirituals are sung with a group of those suffering the same experience. Blues are personal and individually sung.	*These points depict music of the African-American church tradition and aspects common to gospel music.* Music is the core of daily life in Africa, a trait noted in the development of spirituals, blues, and later evident in various genres of black music. We have seen themes of trouble in other black music forms that came along after the blues: gospel, rap, R&B, funk, jazz. Gospel was even birthed out of blues' musical chords. The singer's experience with life is a major contributor to the artistic and authentic ability of all of these. The music of our people all sums up to be "soul" music. It is all sung from the souls of black folk. Black people have a unique way of turning our pains into "gains" in all various aspects of our culture, not just music. We see this in all the black music forms.